General Characteristics of the Germanic Languages

General Characteristics of the Germanic Languages

Antoine Meillet

Translated by William P. Dismuke

The University of Alabama Press

Tuscaloosa

The University of Alabama Press
Tuscaloosa, Alabama 35487-0380
Originally published as *Caractères Généraux des Langues Germaniques*
Copyright © Librairie C. Klincksieck, Paris
English translation copyright © 1970 University of Miami Press
All rights reserved
Manufactured in the United States of America

Published by The University of Alabama Press, 2005

∞

The paper on which this book is printed meets the minimum requirements of
American National Standard for Information Science—Permanence of Paper for
Printed Library Materials, ANSI Z39.48-1984.

Library of Congress Cataloging-in-Publication Data

Meillet, A. (Antoine), 1866–1936.
[Caractères généraux des langues germaniques. English]
General characteristics of the Germanic languages / by Antoine Meillet ; translated
by William P. Dismukes.
p. cm.
Originally published: Coral Gables, Fla.: University of Miami Press, 1970. (Miami
linguistics series ; no. 6)
ISBN-10: 0-8173-5295-3
ISBN-13: 978-0-8173-5295-0 (pbk: alk. paper)
1. Germanic languages—Grammar, Comparative. I. Dismukes, William P. (William Paul), 1903– II. Title. III. Miami linguistics series ; no. 6.

PD101.M413 2004
430'.045—dc22

2005050580

Contents

Preface

EVERY LANGUAGE of the Indo-European group has its own character. Linguists have tried to show how each language can be explained by means of the Indo-European elements which have been revealed in it through comparative grammar. It is no less useful to point out the originality of the various languages. The object of the present little work is to show how the development of the Germanic languages is distinctive among all the Indo-European languages.

There has been no effort to explain all the facts of phonetics and grammar; I have tried only to bring out the innovations which have given the Germanic group a special aspect.

Germanic unity existed only before the historic period. When, at various periods, the Germanic languages became fixed by writing, they were already distinct from one another. Ever since, they have continued to become more and more divergent. A work which deals with Germanic languages in general must therefore be concerned with the most ancient forms of these languages, because these forms are the nearest to the period of unity.

No matter how distinct and independent they may be, the Germanic languages in their developments have remained parallel, because they have been directed by initial changes which were produced during the period of unity. To examine the ancient period of Germanic is then to explain already in part the present state of the group. A constant effort has been made to show how the development leads from the still very archaic type of common Germanic to the quite modern type of English.

I thank the friends who have been good enough to look over the proofs of this work and who have helped me with their advice.

Mr. R. Gauthiot, who was anxious to examine all of this little book, was only able to read the introduction. Death deprived me of his advice for the rest.

Messrs. Maurice Cahen, M. Grammont, and J. Vendryes have each read a proof and have supplied a number of corrections; Mr. Jules Bloch and Mr. Marcel Cohen, who are in the armed forces but who have been

willing to read proofs, have sent me useful comments from their trenches
and from their cantonments at the front.

November 11, 1916

Published during the war, this little book could not take into account
certain publications. Nevertheless, there does not seem to be a need for
much revision, for the litigious questions were deliberately neglected.

In this new edition, changes have been limited to the correction of
mistakes, to the modification of wording in certain places, and to a few
additions, in particular a little chapter on word composition.

September 1922

This new edition did not call for great changes. There have been some
corrections of detail owing largely to a revision made by Mr. Maurice
Cahen.

This edition was in press when I received the article from *The Germanic
Review*, Vol. I, pp. 47–71, in which Mr. E. Prokosch discusses and rejects
the hypothesis that the action of a non-Indo-European "substratum"
explains the special characteristics of Germanic. Even after the objections
of Mr. E. Prokosch, the theory seems to me sound. To judge the action of
a substratum in the matter of pronunciation or grammar, it is sufficient
to observe the forms of Parisian French in southern France where it is a
borrowed idiom. Germanic phonology is an Indo-European phonology,
transposed into a system of foreign habits and foreign tendencies. Each
Indo-European language lends itself, more or less clearly, to similar
observations.

A. M.
March 1926

Except for corrections of detail, owing in part to indications from
Mr. F. Mossé, the fourth edition is a reproduction of the third.

A. M.
January 1930

Abbreviations

In works on comparative grammar, it is customary to place an abridged indication before each word of the language to which it belongs. Most of these abbreviations are clear and easily interpreted, but here is a list of the ones used:

Arm.	Armenian	OHG.	Old High German
Celt.	Celtic	OI.	Old Icelandic
Fr.	French	OIr.	Old Irish
Ger.	German	OLat.	Old Latin
Germ.	Germanic	OPr.	Old Prussian
Got.	Gothic	OR.	Old Russian
Gr.	Greek	OS.	Old Saxon
IE.	Indo-European	OSl.	Old Slavic
Ir.	Irish	OSw.	Old Swedish
Lat.	Latin	Sl.	Slavic
Lit.	Lithuanian	Skr.	Sanskrit
OE.	Old English	Ved.	Vedic
OFr.	Old Frisian	WGerm.	West Germanic

Other abbreviations refer to grammatical terms:

acc.	accusative	nom.	nominative
dat.	dative	part.	participle
fem.	feminine	pers.	person
gen.	genitive	pl.	plural
ind.	indicative	pres.	present
inf.	infinitive	pret.	preterite
masc.	masculine	sg.	singular

Introduction

THE GERMANIC group of languages belongs to the Indo-European language family. But, among these languages, it presents a very distinctive aspect.

There is general agreement in terming "Indo-European" all the languages which, like Indo-Iranian, Greek, Latin, Celtic, and Slavic, are transformations of a common original called Indo-European.

The common origin of these languages is attested by the fact that they correspond in many respects; and it is by observing the correspondences that one succeeds in restoring hypothetically, by a reliable method, the common, nonattested original of the various Indo-European languages. The comparative grammar of Indo-European languages has as its prime purpose the establishment of the theory of these correspondences.

However, in the attested forms of the languages of the group, the corresponding traits are only survivals. None of these languages, not even the dialects fixed by writing for the longest time, offers an exact and complete image of the Indo-European system. The Vedas and the Gathas of the Avesta offer the Indo-Iranian type already fully developed, the Vedas under Indian form, the Gathas under Iranian form; the Homeric poems are altogether Greek. Now, these are by far the most ancient monuments of the Indo-European languages and the most archaic.

From the earliest date, each of the languages of the group exhibits a system of its own. The elements with which this system has been constructed are Indo-European, but the system is new. It is fitting therefore to examine each language in the pursuit of evidence of its special characteristics.

One must not stop at accomplished changes. Changes which have taken place are interesting insofar as they serve as points of departure for the continuation of the history of the language. However, it is the tendencies which direct the development that one must look for before anything else; one must recognize, so to speak, the active principles of change. We limit ourselves too often to observing that to a certain state of things in Indo-European corresponds another state in a given language. The changes which are produced result almost always from general tendencies. These tendencies act before they become manifest, and they continue to act long after their first manifestation. We must refer the changes back to the tendencies from which they proceed. Undoubtedly, the detail of actions will be overlooked; but the general lines are more important than the detail.

Languages are all the more interesting to observe from this point of view because the innovations which they have undergone are more essential and affect more extensively the ensemble of the system. Germanic, which has dislocated the Indo-European system and which has created for itself a new pronunciation and a new grammar, may conserve as many elements of Indo-European as one may wish to find; it is nevertheless a different language from Indo-European. A linguistics which persists in determining the Indo-European origin of each of the smallest elements of Germanic without bringing out the principles of novelty in this group of languages remains attached to curiosities of minor importance and neglects the essentials.

Leaving details aside as much as possible, I should like here to mark the main features of the development of the Germanic languages. This development began long before the attestation of Germanic by written documents, and it has continued for the most part throughout the historical period; in part at least, the developmental tendencies considered continue to act today and give to the Germanic languages a distinctive character among Indo-European languages. In separating prehistoric facts from those of later periods, one often dissociates events which are ascribable to the same tendency: many occurrences which were in the process of development at the date of the earliest texts and which began to be produced before the moment at which these texts were fixed, have materialized only later, some quite recently. Several of the tendencies toward change continue today to produce their effects. These are the tendencies which I wish to bring out.

The Indo-European languages called Germanic are those which in the forms evident in their most ancient documents, as in the tendencies of their development, show certain innovations.

These common innovations and these common tendencies, which are numerous and characteristic, imply that the languages called Germanic are transformations of a particular form of Indo-European. It is this idiom which we shall agree to call "common Germanic." This language is known only by comparing the various Germanic languages, and it is impossible to verify it in the same way that we are able to verify Vulgar Latin from which the Romance languages are descended.

We shall abstain from seeking here where and when the idiom thus designated was spoken; as for the place, one may think of the central part of Europe, perhaps the northern plains of Germany; as for the time, one will not go far wrong in thinking of the two or three centuries before the beginning of the Christian era. Historical data are lacking, however, and it would be imprudent to try to be more precise.

Germanic languages may be divided into three groups: Gothic, Scandinavian, and West Germanic.

The Gothic group has certainly been important. However, the Goths, of a conquering temperament, scattered far beyond their original domain. They created kingdoms in Spain, France, Italy, and the Balkans. Venturing far, they became absorbed, after brilliant successes, by the populations over whom they had established for a brief time their domination. Their language has thus disappeared everywhere. In the sixteenth century, some words of Gothic origin still persisted in Crimea; but there, too, Gothic has gone out of use. Nowhere is there today a population which uses Gothic speech. Except for the proper names of Gothic chiefs, we should be entirely ignorant of Gothic if the Gothic bishop Ulfila had not translated in the fourth century the holy books of Christianity, founding thus a Gothic literary language, and if important fragments of this translation, especially fragments of the New Testament, and also a few small pieces composed in the same language had not been preserved. When one speaks of Gothic, one means therefore the language that Bishop Ulfila fixed in written form. Done in the Balkan Peninsula from a Greek original, his translation has the character of Eastern translations: the author has constituted an alphabet to note the sounds of Gothic, and he has posed regular and constant forms. There is nothing in all Germanic as regular as Gothic because it is a literary language created by a cultivated man at a given moment, based on a given speech pattern.

By reason of the relatively remote date at which it was fixed, the Gothic of Ulfila offers one of the most archaic forms of Germanic. However, Gothic, the language of a migrant and conquering people, was in the fourth century a dialect relatively advanced in its development; many other Germanic dialects of the same period were more conservative. The Gothic of the fourth century had already effaced certain ancient Germanic peculiarities which were still current in the Scandinavian and West Germanic texts of a much later date.

The Scandinavian group, also called Nordic, has been maintained up to the present, and the three dialects which the most ancient monuments reveal are represented in the present by Norwegian (and Icelandic), Swedish, and Danish.

For these three dialects, we have inscriptions in a special alphabet used by the Germanic peoples and known as the runic alphabet. The most ancient inscriptions are perhaps from the third century A.D., but the use of the runic alphabet was continued for a long time and had not yet ceased in the thirteenth century. The old runic inscriptions are short for the most part and often obscure; insofar as they provide linguistic testimony, they are invaluable. For the Nordic of the fourth and fifth centuries A.D. had preserved a very archaic character, and the language of the first runic inscriptions is by far the closest to common Germanic; it is perceptibly more archaic than the Gothic of the same date. The finals are better preserved; where the Gothic has the nominative *gasts*, 'host,' the old runic Norse still has -*gastirr*, with -*i*- as in Latin *hostis*; where Gothic has *stain*, 'stone,' with the final entirely lost, old runic Norse has *staina*.

After the eleventh century there are manuscripts in the three principal Scandinavian dialects.

The first great literary language to be constituted among the Nordic dialects was that of Iceland, a colony of Norway; it produced a gre.. literature from the twelfth to the fourteenth centuries. Hence the form in which ancient Nordic is ordinarily cited is that furnished by the manuscripts of Icelandic literary works of this period; it is what is called Old Icelandic.

The Western group is less unified than the Nordic group. It includes the English group, to which the Frisian dialects are closely related, and the German group, in which we distinguish High German, Low German or Saxon, and Dutch.

It is the group in which the earliest documents are the least ancient. We begin to know Old English, in the beginning especially from glosses, only from the seventh century, Old High German only from the eighth century, and Old Saxon only from the ninth.

Moreover, during the whole ancient period no literary language was developed in any of these domains. In England, the texts present very diverse linguistic forms. As for Old High German, nothing is less unified: there are hardly two texts which show the same aspect; the divergences among the Alemannic, Bavarian, and Franconian writings are marked; moreover, no tradition being fixed, each author or each copyist took into account, to a certain degree, the state of the language at his time and in his region. The name Old High German is applied then to diverse forms written in the High German domain from the eighth to the twelfth centuries especially in the monasteries, just as the name Old English is applied to forms employed in England from the seventh to the twelfth centuries. But there is no unity comparable to that of Gothic or even to that of Old Icelandic.

This situation stems from the fact that in the Western Germanic domain the written language of the scholars was Latin. Germanic expressions were written at first only to gloss the Latin.

Precise historical data are lacking for determining where and how these three well-defined groups were formed. The Germanic-speaking populations were very active and eager for conquests, and, from the moment they appear in history, they strive to extend their domain. There is then in the territory occupied by the three groups at the beginning of the historical period a large measure of conquered land and consequently a large contingent of assimilated populations among those using these three dialects.

The way in which the language is recorded during the ancient periods of each dialect is obviously trustworthy, and one can rely in general on the forms given in the runic inscriptions and in the oldest texts, whether they be Gothic, Scandinavian, or West Germanic. The earliest texts preserved are close to the time when the Germanic dialects were reduced to writing for the first time.

Germanic speakers remained for a long time faithful to the Indo-European custom of not writing about things having to do with religion. The old runic inscriptions are of a profane or magical character; many of them are epitaphs. The first texts we possess are Christian, whether they be from among the Goths who made a translation of the Bible, according to the Eastern usage, or from among the German and English peoples who wrote works of edification. The texts of Old High German are products of the monasteries. The epic literature of Iceland dates from a time when the conversion to Christianity was completed. It is probable that among the ancient Germans writing was introduced slowly. This must have been to some degree intentional, for the Germans were in contact with peoples who wrote. Neither the runic inscriptions nor the first texts, all Christian, bear clearly the trace of their ancient culture.

It seems that everywhere, and notably in the Western domain, the ancient notations of the Germanic dialects are sincere and ingenuous. Unfortunately the runic alphabet of twenty-four characters only permitted approximate and imperfect indications; and notations made with the aid of the Latin alphabet, poorly adapted to the pronunciation of Germanic dialects, are awkward and incoherent. Gothic alone has been recorded in a systematic, carefully thought-out manner.

Thanks to the multiplicity of dialect forms, we are able to get a rather complete idea of what "common Germanic" was like. However, while comparing the forms attested by the oldest texts of the various dialects, we must never lose sight of the fact that the Germanic dialects were in a state of rapid evolution at the beginning of the historical period and that they continued to evolve rapidly. Judging by the earliest runic and Gothic inscriptions, we can assume that common Germanic was very archaic. With relation to Indo-European, many important changes had already taken place, but many others were only being initiated. The tendencies which were to lead to a profound transformation of the language existed, but they had not yet brought about perceptible realizations.

The common Germanic forms reconstituted by the comparison of dialects are often quite divergent from those of the most ancient texts. Take, for example, the nominative Got. *stains*, OI. *steinn*, OE. *stān*, OS. *stēn*, and OHG. *stein*, 'stone'; the runic Norse form, which is *stainaR*, and a comparison of the ancient borrowings of Finnish from Germanic (Finnish *kuningas*, 'king,' as compared with OS. *kuning*) lead us to assume that **stainaz* is the common Germanic form, although this is not attested anywhere. Gothic and the Finnish borrowings exclude -*R*, which is the final Norse consonant; certain facts about Gothic show that -*s* of Got. *stains* represents an ancient **-z*. The assumed form for common Germanic is then **stainaz*. The final **-az* thus restored is precisely what one expects, for the Indo-European final of the inflection of the type represented by **stainaz* was **-os* (Gr. -*os*, OLat. -*os*), and the Indo-European **o* is represented by the Germ. **a*, and the **-s* final in Indo-European by the Germ. **-z*. The restoration **stainaz* for common Germanic is confirmed by the fact that it agrees with the form that the general rules of correspondence between Germanic and Indo-European predict.

From the earliest centuries of the Christian era at least, the Germanic dialects—Gothic, Scandinavian, and Western—developed independently. And soon even the groups within the great dialects developed autonomously: the evolution of English dialects became independent of that of German dialects from the time the conquering Angles and Saxons settled in England.

As was to be expected, the identity of the point of departure and the identity of the inherited tendencies of common Germanic determined a parallelism of development among the various Germanic languages. Being independent of one another, these developments often bring about results that differ in detail. We have seen how the same common Germanic form **stainaz*, undergoing everywhere the effect of the tendency to reduce finals (and also to alter diphthongs, as in the *ai* of the first syllable), gave runic Norse *stainaR* (hence OI. *steinn*), Got. *stains*, and WGerm. **stain*, and hence OE. *stān*, OS. *stén*, and OHG. *stein*.

However, it also happens that the parallel but independent development of the Germanic dialects, after the common Germanic period, furnishes identical results. For example, the accusative singular common Germanic *stainan* becomes Got. *stain,* OI. *stein,* OE. *stān,* OS. *stén,* and OHG. *stein.* If we did not have the old runic Norse *staina,* we could not establish directly that a final vowel fell in this form only between the common Germanic period and that of the most ancient texts of each dialect.

Sometimes the reconstitution of the common Germanic form relies on no positively attested form. Thus we have assumed a final *n* in common Germanic *stainan.*

We know that the pre-Germanic final was *-on* from the Gr. *-on,* Old Pr. *-an,* OLat. *-om,* and Skr. *-am;* but no attested form of a substantive of this type brings direct proof that the nasal was still preserved in common Germanic. We are led to consider this hypothesis as the most probable by the fact that in the demonstratives, for example in the form which corresponds to the accusative Gr. *tón,* and the Skr. *tám,* 'this one,' the nasal is maintained; in Gothic it has subsisted before a particle: *þan-a;* and in OHG. the simple form has kept it, simply because it is monosyllabic: *den.* Thus the reconstitution of common Germanic forms sometimes entails a bit of uncertainty.

Moreover, common Germanic did not constitute a perfect unity. Undoubtedly the ensemble of Germanic presents, in relation to Indo-European, many common innovations and common tendencies to innovation which oblige us to recognize its linguistic unity. But linguistic unity does not mean uniformity.

Uniformity would be particularly unlikely in an ancient Indo-European language. Linguistic unity expresses the unity of a nation, and the unity of common Germanic thus expresses the fact that there was at a given moment, during the centuries which preceded the Christian era, a nation having consciousness of its unity and which, for lack of knowledge of the name it gave itself, we shall call here the Germanic nation. But an ancient Indo-European nation did not have unified institutions, nor was it governed by a single ruler. It was composed of an aggregate of peoples, each having its own usages and its own chiefs. And it is thus that the Germanic nation appears in history not as a state directed by a single ruler, but as a group of peoples whose neighbors recognized their unity; they themselves considered themselves related without ever having formed a political unity. Populations thus independent of one another could not have had a rigorously unified language. Even before the Germans dispersed in all directions to seek adventure, Germanic surely showed dialectal differences.

The comparison of the three attested groups of Germanic languages gives us a glimpse of some of these dialectal differences which existed in common Germanic. For example, in the second-person singular of the preterite indicative of strong verbs, Gothic has *baust*, 'you ordered,' and Old Icelandic has *bautt*; but it is *bude* in Old English, *budi* in Old Saxon, and *buti* in Old High German. This reveals two different types, each of which is irreducible to the other: in Gothic and in Nordic, there is an ending -*t* with the same radical vocalism as in the other persons of the singular; in West Germanic, there is an ending -*i* with the same radical vocalism as in the forms of the plural. These two forms go back to different Indo-European types. Gothic and Nordic have generalized one type, and West Germanic has generalized another, and the difference must go back to the common Germanic period. One glimpses here a line separating the dialectal groups of Germanic. The principal lines of this sort pass between Nordic and Gothic on one side and West Germanic on the other. It seems then that Nordic was a neighbor of the Gothic group, while the West Germanic group was comparatively remote from both Gothic and Scandinavian. However, one must not press this conclusion too far. The facts are neither numerous nor significant, and it would not be legitimate to reduce to two the dialectal groups of Germanic; Gothic is quite distinct from Nordic.

Since the Germanic languages currently spoken have developed independently for many centuries, and since their evolution has almost never ceased to be rapid and at times even abrupt, these languages are now very different from one another. But analogous tendencies have dominated in all of them. German, Dutch, and English are today absolutely different languages, and Danish is very different from Swedish or Norwegian dialects. The degrees to which these languages have diverged from common Germanic are various; but all have evolved in the same direction.

The extreme limit of development is seen in modern English. The ancient finals of words are so reduced that almost nothing remains; the accented part of words is about all that subsists. Hence, the ancient Indo-European morphology is destroyed. Present-day English is an Indo-European language insofar as it is linked to Indo-European without a break in continuity by an uninterrupted series of people who have had the impression of continuing to speak and the will to continue to speak like those who preceded them. However, if we consider only the linguistic type in itself, and disregard the continuity which is an historical fact without current reality, we can see that nothing is farther from the Indo-European type than the English—or the Danish—of today. If, considering present-day English and forgetting the past, we were supposed to demonstrate that English is an Indo-European language, we should have difficulty in succeeding.

I shall not try here to trace the particular development of a given Germanic language. But it is important to note from the beginning that the development of Germanic has consisted of moving farther and farther away from the Indo-European type, up to the point where, as in English and in Danish, almost all trace of this type has disappeared and where one is in the presence of a new linguistic type.

We do not have the means of recognizing with precision the conditions which have determined the progressive change of the type. The linguist states the facts, follows their development, and becomes aware of the procedures by which the changes are made, and he sees how these changes succeed each other and often determine one another. However, the origin of the tendencies to which the changes are owing escapes him.

Certain principles of change are universal; for example, one will not be surprised to see the tendency to reduce the finals, to see intervocalic consonants undergo the influence of neighboring vowels and thus be made like them by becoming voiced or by losing a part of their closure, or, in what concerns grammar, to find the luxuriant complexity of Indo-European inflection becoming simplified. These are universal tendencies; their effects are found in varying degrees in all of the languages of the Indo-European family. In this regard, the only things particular about any one language are the degree of rapidity with which these tendencies act and the detail of the changes.

There are also tendencies which are peculiar to certain languages. Germanic phonetics offers several tendencies of this kind which characterize Germanic in a conspicuous way. The system of consonants, the way in which the vowels are treated, and the nature and place of the accent are traits which specifically characterize the direction Germanic has taken in its departure from Indo-European.

Now, when a population changes language, it is inclined to keep in the newly adopted language some anterior linguistic habits or to modify the type it adopts. Germanic, which has broken so decidedly with Indo-European usages, is Indo-European spoken by a new population which has accepted Indo-European while pronouncing it in a manner partly new. The conquerors who brought Indo-European were neither numerous nor powerful enough to impose their manner of articulation; the people whom they conquered, and who adopted their language, thus caused a different articulatory type and other new tendencies to prevail.

The profound alteration of the grammatical system is undoubtedly owing also to the fact that the new population which adopted the dialect destined to become Germanic did not completely assimilate the grammatical procedures of Indo-European; these procedures, strangely original and complicated, were moreover difficult to learn, and, over the whole extent of the Indo-European domain, one can observe their elimination one after another. Nowhere has the movement which tended to take from the Indo-European type its most characteristic features been more pronounced than in Germanic, just as nowhere else has the Indo-European articulatory type been more completely transformed.

The importance and the rapidity of changes are not owing only to the maintenance of habits anterior to the acceptance of a new language: the most original traits of the newly adopted language are not well assimilated simply because they are too subtle and poorly perceived. Moreover, the various subjects learn the new language unequally, and a great diversity is produced in the linguistic community. There is necessarily a reaction to this diversity; the reaction tends to normalize, and consequently to vulgarize by effacing peculiarities.

In the Germanic group, the forces of linguistic conservation were as slight as possible and remained slight for a long time.

In a unified and stable population, the language participates in the general stability; where everyone speaks more or less the same dialect, each individual is induced to conform to general usage, and all deviations are condemned and ridiculed. Now, from the time of their appearance in history, the Germanic populations have been conquerors. Some ventured too far and became absorbed by other populations; this is what happened to the Goths, to the Germanic tribes who passed into France, to the Scandinavians who went to Ireland, Normandy, or Russia, and to many others. Those who were more resistant imposed their idiom on the peoples among whom they settled; this is what happened notably in England. Conquests of this sort are followed by troubled periods during which there is scarcely any linguistic uniformity and, consequently, a minimum of resistance to change.

A true national civilization preserved by an intellectual aristocracy fixes the linguistic ideal and contributes thus to maintaining the ancient type. Now, the Germans encountered a more advanced civilization, the Greco-Roman, and they were strongly influenced by it even before the beginning of the Christian era. Many of them served in the Roman armies. The national civilization was thus invaded by foreign elements: the runic alphabet, special though it is, comes from northern Italy, as Mr. C. Marstrander has observed. It yielded when Christianity was introduced; thereupon Greek and Latin became the learned languages, and the Germanic dialects served only for colloquial use.

A truly unified empire tends to give itself a common language which will serve as an organ. Now, there were Germanic tribes which made conquests, and there were also Germanic kingdoms, but these were not very durable for the most part and were very quickly replaced; at no period then does history present a Germanic empire. The greatest of the Germanic conquerors, Charlemagne, appears quite late. Moreover, he was far from successful in uniting under his authority all the Germany of his time. As Mr. C. Jullian has remarked, the civilization he protected and developed was not one of Germanic language: the Carolingian renaissance was, as is well known, a renaissance of Latin studies. Prior to the period, the ninth to the fourteenth centuries, when strongly differentiated national languages began to appear, the Germanic-speaking populations did not have a Germanic language of civilization. The Germanic dialects served for household use, for everyday social relations; they had no norm maintained by a learned tradition. The rapidity with which English evolved during the period of Norman domination, when French was the language of the court, of the nobility, and of the writers, shows the extent to which a language deprived of an ideal norm can be transformed.

Even when literary languages were constituted, in the Middle Ages these were not the languages of scholars. They were used for poetry, and their influence on speech was slight, especially in the English and German domains.

I should like to show here what directions Indo-European followed to become common Germanic, and how, in turn, from common Germanic were formed the Gothic, Nordic, and Western types, the latter two of which gave rise to the modern Germanic languages. Although often broken by accidents, the lines of this development present, as we shall see, a remarkable continuity on the whole.

It will not be a question of rediscovering Indo-European in the Germanic dialects. The object of this little book is, on the contrary, to show in what way Germanic is original. The materials with which Germanic is formed are Indo-European; the plan of the language is new. To tell the truth, each of the languages of the Indo-European group had developed its own characteristics by the date at which it first appears in history. However, nowhere can one see better than in Germanic how an Indo-European language is a new creation, and is for that very reason interesting.

PART ONE

PHONOLOGY

Chapter I

The Mutation of Consonants

THE INDO-EUROPEAN consonant system was rich and complete in occlusives, but it possessed no spirants except a sibilant *s; the *z existed only as the form taken by *s before a voiced occlusive. The essentially voiced phonemes, which are often called semivowels, and which we shall call "sonant consonants," *y, w, r, l, m, and n, are not to be examined in the present chapter.

In the Western group of Indo-European dialects, of which Germanic forms a part, the system of occlusives contained four types: the labial type, for example *p; the dental type, for example *t; the guttural type, for example *k; and the labiovelar type, for example *kʷ (which can also be indicated by qʷ). Each of these four types existed in three series: the voiceless series, *p, t, k, and kʷ; the voiced series, *b, d, g, and gʷ; and the voiced aspirated series (as shown in the Sanskrit series), *bh, dh, gh, and gʷh. If we judge by Indo-Iranian, Greek, and Armenian, it appears that another less important series of voiceless aspirated occlusives existed: ph, th, and kh; but this series is not distinguished from the ordinary voiceless series in Germanic, Celtic, and Italic and consequently will be neglected here.

The consonant system of common Germanic is quite different. It retains the same points of articulation, but it has new articulatory types. It includes voiceless occlusives, *p, t, k, and kʷ (qʷ), and voiced occlusives, *b, d, g, and gʷ, which were perhaps aspirated voiced occlusives. On the other hand, one finds a series of voiceless spirants: *f (bilabial), þ, x, and xʷ; and a series of voiced spirants: *ƀ, d, γ, γʷ (which becomes simply *w). Beside the sibilant *s, there is a *z which is not always owing to the influence of a following voiced occlusive.[1]

We shall see in Chapter II that the voiced spirants *ƀ, d, γ, and γʷ (which becomes *w), as well as *z, are forms taken by *b, d, g, and gʷ,

1. We shall note here by þ the voiceless dental spirant of the type of English th in a word like thing; by d the voiced dental spirant of the type of English th in the interior of words, as in mother; by x the voiceless guttural spirant of the type of German ch, as in doch; by γ the voiced guttural spirant (that one hears, for example, at the end of German tag).

and by $*f$, $þ$, x, x^w, and $*s$ under definite conditions. This first chapter will discuss only the voiceless spirants $*f$, $þ$, x, and x^w. The introduction of these spirants into the phonetic system is at first the most striking innovation.

If, instead of comparing systems, one examines the origin of each of the series of common Germanic consonants, the Germanic innovation appears much more important. Indeed:

1. Germanic voiceless consonants do not represent Indo-European voiceless consonants, but simple Indo-European voiced consonants: Germ. $*p$, t, k, and k^w correspond to Skr. b, d, j, and g (which alternates with j under certain conditions), Gr. b, d, g, and b (which alternates with d or g under certain conditions), Lat. b, d, g, and g^w (and u consonant), Celt. b, d, g, and b, Sl. b, d, z, and g (which alternates with $ž$), Lit. b, d, $ž$, and g, and so forth.

2. The Germanic spirants $*f$, $þ$, x, and x^w represent IE. $*p$, t, k, and k^w, and correspond to Lat. p, t, k (c), and qu; Gr. p, t, k, and p (which alternates with t or k under certain conditions); Lit. p, t, sz (which indicates $š$), and k; Sl. p, t, s, and k (which alternates with $č$); Skr. p, t, $ç$, and k (which alternates with c, which in turn indicates the semiocclusive $č$), and so forth. Very early $*x$ tended to lose its spirant character and to become a simple breath h, a tendency which is not peculiar to Germanic (one observes analogous occurrences in Latin and Serbian for example); as far back as the earliest texts in all the Germanic languages, then, we find h where the common Germanic had $*x$, and hw where the common Germanic had $*x^w$.

3. The Germanic voiced consonants $*b$, d, g, and g^w represent IE. $*bh$, dh, gh, and g^wh, and correspond to Skr. bh, dh, h, gh (which alternates with h), Gr. ph, th, kh, and ph (which alternates with th or kh), Lat. f (ancient $*f$ and $*þ$), h (ancient x), and f (ancient x^w), and so forth.

Except for the sibilant $*s$ and the voiced aspirated consonants (if Germ. $*b$ is bh), there is no properly called Germanic consonant which has remained in the series in which it was in Indo-European. That is what one means when one says that the Indo-European occlusives have undergone in Germanic a "mutation" (called in German *Lautverschiebung*). The discovery of this great occurrence was published in 1818 by the Dane P. K. Rask and in 1822 by the German Jacob Grimm; the principle has often been called "Grimm's Law."

When we bring together Germanic words and the corresponding words in Sanskrit, Greek, Latin, Celtic, Slavic, and so on, we notice that Germanic consonants with the exception of $*s$ are never identical with those of Sanskrit, Greek, Latin, and the other languages; there are exceptions only in well-determined cases which can be explained as will be seen below. The identities which we observe with certain languages, such as Celtic, Baltic, Slavic, and Iranian, have to do only with the ancient voiced aspirated consonants and result from the fact that like Germanic these languages represent by *b*, *d*, and *g* the Indo-European voiced aspirated occlusives *bh*, *dh*, and *gh*; but, unlike Germanic, these languages which preserve the ancient simple voiced occlusives confuse them with the ancient voiced aspirated occlusives.

Here are a few examples of etymological correspondences which will illustrate the principles stated:

1. Ancient voiced sounds represented by Germanic voiceless sounds:

   b > *p*:
Lit. *dubùs*, 'deep'; cf. Got. *diups*, OI. *diūpr*, OE. *dēop*.

   d > *t*:
Skr. *dántam*, 'tooth,' Lat. *dentem*; cf. Got. *tunþu*, OE. *tōd*, OS. *tand* (all of these words are cited in the accusative singular).

Skr. *pádam*, 'foot,' Gr. *póda*, Lat. *pedem*; cf. Got. *fotu*, OI. *fōt*, OE. *fōt* (all of these words are cited in the accusative singular).

   g > *k*:
Skr. *jánu*, 'knee,' Gr. *góny*, Lat. *genu*; cf. Got. *kniu*, OE. *knēo*.

Skr. *ájraḥ*, 'country,' Gr. *agrós*, 'field,' Lat. *ager*; cf. Got. *akrs*, OI. *akr*, OS. *akkar*.

   gʷ > *kʷ*:
Skr. *gná*, 'woman,' OPr. *genna*, OSl. *žena*, Beotian Gr. *baná* (and Attic Gr. *gynế*); cf. Got. *qino*, OHG. *quena*.

2. Ancient voiced aspirated occlusives represented by Germanic voiced occlusives perhaps aspirated:

   bh > *b*:
Skr. *bhárāmi*, 'I bear,' Gr. *phérō*, Lat. *ferō*; cf. Got. *bairan*, 'to carry,' OI. *bera*, WGerm. *beran*.

   dh > *d*:
Skr. *dhṛṣṇóti*, 'he dares,' *dhṛṣúḥ*, 'bold,' Gr. *thrasýs*, 'bold'; cf. Got. *(ga-)dars*, 'he dares,' OE. *dear(r)*.

   gh > *g*:
Skr. *haṃsáḥ* (a kind of wild aquatic bird), Gr. *khến*, 'goose,' Lat. *(h)anser*, Lit. *žąsis*; cf. OI. *gās*, OE. *gōs*, OHG. *gans*.

gʷh > ?: No sure example at the beginning of a word. There is no certain example except for the intervocalic position, which will be examined in Chapter II.

3. Ancient voiceless occlusives represented by voiceless spirants in Germanic:

$*p > *f$ (bilabial):

Ved. *páçu*, 'cattle,' Lat. *pecu*; cf. Got. *faihu*, OI. *fē*, OE. *feoh*, OHG. *fihu*.

Skr. *nápāt*, 'descendant,' Lat. *nepōs*, 'grandson, nephew'; cf. OI. *nefe*, 'relative, nephew,' OE. *nefa*, OHG. *nefo*.

$*t > *þ$:

Ved. *trí*, 'three,' Gr. *tría*, Lat. *tria*; cf. Got. *þrija*, OI. *þriū*, OE. *drēo*, OS. *thriu* (in the neuter nominative-accusative plural).

Skr. *vártate*, 'he turns,' Lat. *uertō*; cf. Got. *wairþan*, 'to become,' OE. *weordan*, OS. *werthan*.

$*k > *x > *h$:

Skr. *çatám*, 'hundred,' Lat. *centum*, Gr. *-katón* (*he-katón*, 'one hundred'); cf. Got. *hund*, OE. *hund*, OHG. *hunt*.

$*k^w > *x^w > *hw$:

Skr. *kataráh*, 'which of the two,' Lit. *katràs*, Gr. *póteros*; cf. Got. *hwaþar*, OI. *huaþarr*, OE. *hwæder*, OS. *hwedar*, OHG. *hwedar*.

Lit. *lēkù*, 'I leave,' Gr. *leipō* (and Lat. *linquō*, *liqui*); cf. Got. *leihwan*, 'lend.'

After *s*, the ancient voiceless occlusives are represented by voiceless occlusives in Germanic; to Skr. *spaç-*, 'spy,' and Lat. *speciō*, 'I look,' correspond OHG. *speho*, 'spy,' and *spehōn*, 'to observe'; to Skr. *stṛbhíh*, 'by the stars' (instrumental plural), and Gr. *astḗr*, correspond Got. *stairno*, OI. *stiarna*, and OHG. *sterno*. Likewise to *pt*, *kt*, and so on, Germanic corresponds with *ft* and *xt*, meaning that in a group of voiceless occlusives, the first will be a spirant, the second an occlusive. Thus, to Skr. *naptíh*, 'little girl,' and Lat. *neptis* corresponds OE. and OHG. *nift*; to Skr. *aṣṭaú* (ancient *ak 'tāú*, 'eight') and Lat. *octō* correspond Got. *ahtau*, OE. *eahta*, and OHG. *ahto*.

In both the cases of a voiceless occlusive preceded by *s* and of one preceded by another voiceless occlusive, the passage to the spirant pronunciation has been prevented by a preceding phoneme. We can form hypotheses concerning the way in which the alteration has been prevented only after having seen by what intermediaries the language arrived at the spirant pronunciation.

The facts thus recognized remain to be interpreted. Germanic is not the only Indo-European language in which we observe a mutation. Armenian offers a mutation almost entirely parallel. The ancient voiced aspirated consonants are represented by voiced phonemes: *berem*, 'I bear,' corresponding to Skr. *bhárāmi*, Gr. *phérō*, and Got. *baira*; the ancient simple voiced phonemes are represented by voiceless ones: *kin*, 'woman,' corresponding to Ved. *gná*, OPr. *genna*, and Got. *qino*; finally, the ancient simple voiceless occlusives are represented by voiceless aspirated occlusives (often altered in various ways): *khan*, 'than,' corresponding to Lat. *quam* (with the same meaning).

This treatment of voiceless occlusives in Armenian indicates the means by which the same occlusives became spirants in Germanic: the first stage of change must have been from simple voiceless occlusives to aspirated voiceless occlusives, from *$*k$* to *$*kh$* for example.

To pass from the occlusive *$*kh$* to the spirant x there are two possibilities. The aspirated voiceless occlusives are in general more weakly articulated than the corresponding nonaspirated ones; they lose then their occlusion rather easily, and from occlusives become spirants. This change is observed in various circumstances in Latin, Irish (in intervocalic position), and Aramaic (also in intervocalic position). In German we observe another process: the *$*p$* of common Germanic becomes *pf*, a type called "affricated," as we shall see below; *pf* can become *f*, which is what happened in German for the intervocalic position. Thus *slēpan*, 'to sleep,' *$*slāpan$* in West Germanic, changed to *$*slāpfan$* and then to OHG. *slāffan*. It is most probable that the common Germanic change was realized by the first process, for there does not exist any trace of the affricated type among the phonemes which represent IE. *$*p$*, *t*, and *k*, and the process of affrication, not widespread in general, is observed only in the later development of certain Germanic dialects, especially the High German dialects.

This granted, the Germanic change and the Armenian change—which are independent of one another—can be reduced to the same general formula.

There are two types of articulation of occlusives distinguished by the behavior of the glottis.

In one of the types, which is found notably in almost all of the Romance languages, particularly French, and in the Slavic languages, the glottis is as closed as possible and ready to articulate the following vowel from the moment the consonant ceases. The voiceless occlusives are then pronounced with the glottis closed; as a result, during the closing of the organs of occlusion, from the moment of "implosion" to the moment of "explosion," no air is accumulated behind the organ whose opening produces the characteristic noise of the consonant, and the glottal vibrations of the following vowel begin immediately after the explosion of the consonant. As for the voiced occlusives, they are accompanied by glottal vibrations during the entire period of occlusion. Thus the *pa* of French does not include any emission of air between the *p* and the *a*; the French *ba* is voiced from the moment the lips are brought together to form the *b*.

In the other type, which is observed notably in the northern German dialects and in certain Armenian dialects, the voiceless occlusives are pronounced with the glottis incompletely closed during the period of occlusion; air is accumulated in the mouth during the period of occlusion, and this air must be expelled after the explosion of the occlusive. The voiceless occlusives of this type, where the emission of breath is interspersed between the explosion of the consonant and the beginning of the vowel, are called "aspirated." For the voiced occlusives *b*, *d*, and *g*, there is a corresponding mode of articulation: the glottal vibrations begin only at the moment of the explosion, and the whole period of occlusion is voiceless; but these occlusives are distinguished from the French type of voiceless phonemes by the weakness of the articulation; they are lenis, not fortis.

In short, what distinguishes the occlusives of this second type from those of the first type is the delayed action of the glottis with reference to the moment of the explosion of the occlusive. For the voiceless occlusives, the glottis closes later; for the voiced, it begins to vibrate later.

Therefore, the change of the Indo-European type to the common Germanic type or to the Armenian type consists of a change from the type in which the glottis acts from the moment of the implosion to a type in which the glottis enters into action only at the moment of the explosion of the consonant. This is a radical change in the articulatory type. It has affected the ancient voiceless $*p$, t, k, and k^w, and the ancient voiced $*b$, d, g, and g^w, which have become respectively $*ph$, th, kh, and k^wh (voiceless aspirated), and $*p$, t, k, and k^w (voiceless lenis). In Germanic as in Armenian, this change has spared the ancient aspirated voiced occlusives because these consonants were produced with a special glottal articulation of the voiced type, the exact nature of which is not known; thus $*bh$, dh, and gh have been represented by $*b$, d, and g, which were undoubtedly aspirated in the beginning in the two languages.

The geminate voiceless occlusives, fortis by nature, were undoubtedly pronounced with the closing of the glottis from the moment of the implosion, which is strongly marked; and consequently we have -*tt*- in Got. *atta*, 'father,' which corresponds to Lat. *atta* and Gr. *átta*, 'papa.' This treatment is peculiar to the geminate type with expressive value.

Where the group $*$-*tt*- results from the encounter of two morphologic elements, it has undergone, from the time of Indo-European, an alteration and appears under the form -*st*- in Iranian, Slavic, Baltic, and Greek, and under the form -*ss*- in the Western dialects—Italic, Celtic, and Germanic. For example, $*wit$-*to*-, 'known,' in which the root $*wid$-, 'to know,' is combined with the suffix *-to-*, becomes *-wistos* in Greek, but in Irish it is *fess* and in Germanic *wissa-* (OHG. *giwisso*, 'certainly,' and Got. *un-wiss*, 'uncertain').

In Armenian, *t* and *p* have not taken, or have not kept, after *s*, the aspirated pronunciation. The same thing is true in present-day Germanic languages. If this was also true in ancient Germanic, the spirant pronunciation did not have to be eliminated since that point of departure did not even exist.

The occlusives of the type with retarded action of the glottis are less stable than the occlusives of the French type. The aspirated voiceless occlusives are likely to become spirants, as has happened in Germanic. The lenis voiceless occlusives, which are somewhere between voiceless and voiced and which appear to Frenchmen to be the effect of poorly executed voiced occlusives (they are often heard among Alsatians and Germans from the south who speak French), tend to become voiceless fortis, and this appears to have occurred early in the Germanic dialects. Nevertheless, *p*, *t*, and *k* remained lenis for a long time: the Latin name for the Greeks, *Graeci*, was borrowed with an initial *k*, which shows that the Germanic *k* was still used at a historic date to render the Latin *g*: Got. *krekos* and OHG. *kriahha*.

The change of **kh* to **x*, and no doubt in a general manner of aspirated voiceless occlusives to spirants, is found in another word which could not be a very ancient borrowing: the name of the Celtic population that the Romans called *volca* (in the nominative masculine singular) is rendered in Germanic by OE. *wealh*, and OHG. *walh*.

Words borrowed by Germanic from Celtic, undoubtedly at the time of the extension of the Celtic empire, between the fifth and the third centuries B.C., underwent consonant mutation: the Celtic word *rig*, 'king,' is rendered in Gothic by *reiks*, from which is derived Got. *reiki*, 'kingdom,' OI. *rike*, OE. *rice*, and OS. *riki*. The consonant mutation no doubt dates then from the centuries which immediately preceded the Christian era.

A change which, like the consonant mutation of Germanic and Armenian, consists of a profound change in the articulatory process, and in particular of the activity of the glottis of which the speaker is not conscious, is naturally explained by the fact that a population, while changing its language, has kept its old articulatory habits: the manner of pronouncing occlusives is one of the most difficult features of pronunciation to change. For Germanic, spoken by a nation whose history begins very late, we cannot say from what population this articulatory type is derived; we shall only note that a neighboring language, Celtic, appears to have undergone an analogous action, and that we find in it a manner of articulating the occlusives which approaches the Germano-Armenian type, without being as absolute. As for Armenia, the introduction of an Indo-European dialect took place at a historic date; and, moreover, the system of Armenian occlusives, which is quite special, is identical with that of a group of neighboring languages, of a different family, the Caucasian group of the south, of which the best-known representative is Georgian. The foreign influence, which theory alone leads us to infer for Germanic, is then indicated by positive facts for Armenian. We may conclude therefrom that the consonant mutation of Germanic is owing to the maintenance of habits of articulation by the populations which received and adopted the Indo-European dialect, called thereafter Germanic.

The new articulatory type once introduced in Germanic continued to produce its effects, which are especially noticeable in High German.

The *b, d,* and *g* of common Germanic did not remain true voiced consonants—no doubt they were voiced aspirated; these voiced aspirated consonants change clearly to a voiceless aspirated pronunciation, as happened in some of the Armenian dialects. In the old Bavarian and Alemannian texts, there is a characteristic wavering between the graphemes *b* and *p*, and *g* and *k*: *beran* and *peran*, 'to carry,' and *guot* and *kuot*, 'good.' In all of the High German dialects, including a part of Franconian, *d* clearly changes to *t*: to Got. *dauhtar*, 'daughter,' and OS. *dohter* (and likewise in a part of Franconian) corresponds OHG. *tohter*.

The common Germanic *p, t,* and *k* tend to become affricated. In Old High German, *p* changes to *pf* and *t* to *z* (which indicates *ts*): to *plegan*, 'to care for,' of Old Saxon corresponds OHG. *pflegan* (except in a part of Franconian), and to OS. *tiohan*, 'to draw,' corresponds OHG. *ziohan*. The *k* was affected only in Bavarian and in Alemannian; the *korn*, 'grain,' of Old Saxon and Franconian is represented in these dialects by *chorn*, with the value of *ch* not being always determinable: there were diverse pronunciations from *kx* to *x*.

Thus there was produced in Old High German a second consonant mutation, a continuation of the phenomena of the first mutation, under slightly different forms. These changes, varying in extent from one German dialect to another, took place between the first century of the Christian era and the time when the oldest High German texts were written; the words borrowed by German from the Latin of the imperial epoch participate in these changes, and Lat. *porta*, for example, becomes OHG. *pforta*, and Lat. *discus* becomes OHG. *tisk*, 'table.'

Germanic spirants were poorly preserved in Old High German; *x* had changed at an early date to *h*; and **f* bilabial became labiodental *f*, which has since been stable. The spirant *þ* became voiced in *d*, and this *d*, sometimes written *dh*, changed to the occlusive pronunciation *d* between the eighth and the tenth centuries, with the exact dates varying in different regions: hence we have *driu*, 'three' (in the neuter), but OS. *thriu*. Thus a *d* has been restored to High German; with *b* and *g*, which have a quite different origin and which continue the common Germanic *b* and *g*, it completes the series of voiced German occlusives. What has made this alteration possible is that the ancient German series *b*, *d*, and *g* was not composed of voiced sounds of the French type.

After all these changes, German has been found to possess, on the one hand, voiced occlusives, *b*, *d*, and *g*, which are pronounced in various ways according to location and which in Alemannian and Bavarian dialects are voiceless lenis, and, on the other hand, voiceless occlusives, *p* (in general in words borrowed recently), *t*, and *k*. The tendency to delay the closing of the glottis has continued to act; *p*, *t*, and *k* tend again to become aspirated. In the domain of High German, the *k* of *korn* and the *t* of *tochter* are now aspirates, so that one can say that in this region there has been the beginning of a third mutation. In reality, the articulatory type once established in common Germanic has been constantly reproduced in High German, and it is a question of a continuous development.

In the other Germanic dialects, the common Germanic type has tended to disappear, and the occlusives have more or less come closer to the Romance type, which is the most stable, the most durable. Thus the occlusives of Low German are almost exactly of the same type as the French occlusives. Things have not gone so far everywhere. The voiceless occlusives of Danish and English are still today more aspirated than those of French. In Danish, we even notice a tendency toward the affrication of the voiceless occlusives: *t* tends toward *ts*, as in Old High German, and the voiced consonants *b*, *d*, and *g* are less completely voiced than those of the Romance and Slavic languages.

After the great disturbance suffered by the system of occlusives in common Germanic, equilibrium was slow in becoming completely reestablished. Except in German and Danish, it has, however, been restored almost everywhere.

In the Celtic group, one finds again at least the beginning of a phenomenon similar to that which had such important consequences in Germanic: the voiceless occlusives in Gaelic and Welsh are of the type called aspirated. But unlike Germanic, the innovation has not gone so far as to produce a complete mutation; the phenomenon has not gone beyond the first stages.

2—GL • •

Chapter II

The Intervocalic Consonants

CONSONANTS PLACED between vowels tend in general to degenerate so as to approach in some measure the vocalic type. Voiceless consonants tend to become voiced, and occlusives tend to become spirants. In Danish, the ancient voiceless intervocalic occlusives have become voiced; *giutan, 'to pour,' is represented by gyde. In modern German, an ancient p is represented by pf initially, as in pflegen from *plegan, but the same p is represented by f when intervocalic, as in schlafen from *slāpan, 'to sleep.' Similarly, t becomes ts initially, as in zehn, from *tehan, 'ten,' but it becomes ss when intervocalic, as in wasser, from *watar, 'water.' Occurrences of this sort are innumerable.

The alteration of intervocalic consonants has affected two series of Germanic consonants: the occlusives *b, d, g, and g^w, which continue, as we have seen, the ancient aspirated voiced occlusives; and, with definite exceptions, the voiceless spirant phonemes, namely the sibilant *s and the voiceless spirants *f, þ, x, and x^w, representing the ancient voiceless occlusives.

The voiced occlusives *b, d, g, and g^w have become spirants between two vowels; thus we have between vowels *ƀ, đ, γ, and w. It is often taught that voiced aspirated occlusives have given voiced spirants in Germanic. However, the spirant pronunciation is attested only for those cases where these consonants are found between two vowels. For example, Old Icelandic records b initially but has f between vowels: bera, 'to carry,' but grafa, 'to dig.' The same is true of Old English: beran, but giefan, 'to give.' Old Saxon, which has b initially, as in beran, fluctuates between b, u, and v between vowels. The Gothic b, like the Greek β of the fourth century A.D., serves to represent both b and ƀ, but a detail shows that the ancient intervocalic b was pronounced as a spirant. In common Germanic, a form such as that of the first and third persons of the preterite had a final vowel, as in *gaƀa, 'I gave,' *gaƀi, 'he gave.' However, the final vowels disappeared, and the ƀ became final. Then, as in Gothic, the final spirants became voiceless, the ƀ became f, and we find the written form gaf, along with giban, 'to give,' gebun, 'they gave,' and so forth. After a nasal, the voiced occlusives do not become spirants, and consequently Gothic has forms such as *lamb*, 'lamb,' with final *b*. The *g^w* is maintained after a nasal; thus Gothic has *siggwan*, 'to sing,' opposite Greek *omphê*, 'voice' (from *$song^wh\bar{a}$*). Between vowels this same *g^w* becomes *w* in Got. *snaiws*, 'snow,' OE. *snā(w)*, and OHG. *sneo*, opposite Lit. *snĕgas*, 'snow,' Gr. *neíphei*, 'it snows,' Lat. *nix (niuis)*, 'snow,' and *ninguit*, 'it snows.'

Germanic has thus created a series of voiced spirants: *b*, *d*, and *γ*. This series has been enriched by the voicing of some of the ancient *f*, *p*, and *x* between vowels.

Moreover, intervocalic *s* has tended to change to *z* in the same conditions where *f*, *p*, and *x* have become voiced in *b*, *d*, and *γ*; and *z*, which was maintained in Gothic, has changed to a phoneme of the type *r* in Nordic and West Germanic. The runic alphabet has for *r* issued from *z* a symbol different from that which records ancient *r* (this sign is transcribed by *R*); hence the fusion of ancient *r* and *r* issued from *z* was not completed by the beginning of the Christian era.

A problem is raised here. Of the ancient *s*, *f*, *p*, *x*, and *x^w*, some remained voiceless in Germanic, while others became *z*, *b*, *d*, *γ*, and *w*, without anything in Germanic which justifies this difference.

The Danish linguist K. A. Verner recognized the principle of the distribution, which is now called "Verner's Law." To clarify the facts established, the formula is presented here in a more restricted and more precise form than that given by K. A. Verner.

The sibilant *s* and the spirants *f*, *p*, *x*, and *x^w* became voiced between two voiced elements, one of which is the vocalic element of the first syllable of the word, when the pitch accent, inherited from Indo-European, falling on this syllable did not prevent the voicing.

To Skr. *pitá* (acc. *pitáram*) and Gr. *patér*, 'father,' Germanic corresponds with Got. *fadar*, OE. *faeder*, OS. *fader*, and OHG. *fater*, forms in which there had been an intervocalic *d*, because, as Sanskrit and Greek show, the Indo-European accent (consisting of an elevation of the voice) did not fall on the first syllable of the word. On the contrary, to Skr. *bhrátā* (acc. *bhrátaram*), 'brother,' and Gr. *phrátēr*, 'member of a brotherhood,' Germanic corresponds with Got. *bropar*, OE. *bróðor*, OS. *bróther*, and OHG. *bruoder*, forms in which there had been an intervocalic *p*, because the Indo-European accent fell on the first syllable. To Skr. *çváçurah* (from *$sv\bar{a}\c{c}urah$*), 'father of the husband,' Germanic corresponds with Got. *swaihra* and OHG. *swehur*, because the accent fell on the initial syllable (the accentuation of Gr. *hekyrós* is secondary); on the contrary, to Skr. *çvaçrúh* (from *$sva\c{c}r\acute{u}h$*), 'mother of the husband,' where the accent is not on the initial, Germanic corresponds with OE. *sweger* and OHG. *swigar*. The *$*k^w$* in the Indo-European word for "wolf," having become *$*x^w$* in Germanic, changed to *$*f$* doubtless under the influence of the initial *$*w$*; *$*f$* persisted because the accent is on the initial syllable: Got. *wulfs*, OI. *ulfr*, OE. and OS. *wulf*, and OHG. *wolf*, opposite Skr. *vŕkaḥ* (the Gr. *lýkos* seems to be the same form). The feminine OI. *ylgr* (where the guttural pronunciation is preserved) has a voiced consonant, which is explained by the ancient position of the accent: cf. Skr. *vṛkíḥ*, 'she-wolf.' The *$*s$* of a word like OE. *nasu* (and *nosu*), 'nose,' persists because the accent was on the initial syllable (cf. Ved. *nā́sā*, 'nostrils'; on the contrary, opposite Skr. *snuṣā́* and Gr. *nyós*, 'daughter-in-law,' we have, with *r* representing a *$*z$* of common Germanic, OI. *snor*, OE. *snoru*, and OHG. *snura*. There is a striking contrast between Got. *taihun*, OS. *tehan*, OHG. *zehan* (from *$*dekṃd$*, *$*dekomd$*), where the ancient voiceless spirant is maintained, as opposed to Lit. *dẽšimt*, 'ten,' and Got. *hund*, OS. *hund*, OHG. *hunt*, 'hundred,' where ancient *$*þ$* changes to *$*d$* (which becomes occlusive after a nasal), and Skr. *çatám*, and Gr. *-katón*, 'hundred.'

In spite of examples of this sort which show the principle of the distribution, we might still doubt the generality of the rule because we know the place of the Indo-European accent only for a very restricted number of words, and, besides, the place of the Indo-European accent varied under complex conditions which are not exactly known. However, certain grammatical facts supply decisive proof.

The preterite of strong verbs is based essentially on the Indo-European perfect. Now, Sanskrit has in the perfect a variation in the position of the accent which must be of considerable antiquity. Unlike singular forms such as Skr *véda*, 'I know, he knows,' which have the accent on the initial syllable, the plural forms *vidmá*, 'we know,' *vidá*, 'you know,' and *vidúḥ*, 'they know,' have the accent on the ending. Germanic presents in its strong preterites an alternation between *$*f$*, *þ*, *x*, *$*x^w$*, and *s* in the singular and *$*b$*, *d*, *γ*, *w*, and *z* (changed to *r* in Nordic and West Germanic) in the plural, which is explained by a variation in the place of the accent agreeing with that of Sanskrit. We have then:

	OI.	OE.	OS.	OHG.
3rd sg.		*tēah*	*tōh*	*zōh*
				'he pulled'
3rd pl.		*tugon*	*tugun*	*zugun*
				'they pulled'

(Cf. Lat. *dūcō*, 'I lead.')

	OI.	OE.	OS.	OHG.
3rd sg.		*weard*		*ward*
				'he became'
3rd pl.		*wurdon*		*wurtun*
				'they became'

(Cf. Skr. *várte*, 'I turn,' Lat. *uertō*.)

	OI.	OE.	OS.	OHG.
3rd sg.		*seah*	*sah*	*sah*
				'he saw'
3rd pl.		*sāwon*	*sāwun*	
				'they saw'

(The intervocalic consonant is **hw*: Got. *saihwan*, 'to see.')

	OI.	OE.	OS.	OHG.
3rd sg.	*vas*	*was*	*was*	*was*
				'he was'
3rd pl.	*vǫro*	*wāeron*	*wārun*	*wārun*
				'they were'

(Cf. Skr. *vásati*, 'he remains.')

Gothic has in general lost these grammatical alternations. However it has preserved a trace of them in its preterite-presents; for example, it opposes *aih*, 'he possesses,' to *aigun*, 'they possess' (cf. Skr. *íçe*, 'I have power over').

Another series of alternations, just as convincing, is furnished by the causative verbs. The presents of the type called "thematic" with radical vowel *e*, the type to which most Germanic strong verbs belong, had the accent on the initial syllable, while the causatives had the accent on the suffix; Sanskrit thus opposes *várdhati*, 'he believes,' to *vardháyati*, 'he causes to believe.' For sibilants and spirants, this is represented in Germanic by alternations between voiceless and voiced pronunciations: Got. *fra-wairþan*, 'to perish' (cf. Skr. *vártate*, 'he turns') but *fra-wardjan*, 'to cause to perish' (cf. Skr. *vartáyati*, 'he causes to turn'). For example, opposite OE. *ge-nesan*, and OS. and OHG. *gi-nesan*, 'to cure' (cf. Skr. *násate*, 'he returns,' and Gr. *néetai*, 'he returns,' beside *nós-tos*, 'return'), we find OE. *nerigan*, OS. *nerian*, and OHG. *nerien*, 'to save' (cf. Skr. *nāsáyati*, 'he causes to return'); Gothic, which preserves the alternations poorly here as in the perfect, has generalized the *s* of *ga-nisan* and consequently has *nasjan*, 'to save.'

The radical adjectives in **-to-* and in **-no-*, which Germanic has incorporated in the verbal system, had the accent on the suffix in Indo-European—thus Skr. *çru-tá-h*, 'understood,' Gr. *kly-tó-s*, 'celebrated,' or Skr. *pur-ņá-h*, 'full.' This is what causes the intervocalic voiceless spirants to become voiced, while the corresponding present has a voiceless inter-vocalic spirant: OS. *tiohan* and OHG. *ziohan*, 'to draw, pull,' but OS. *gi-togan* and OHG. *gizogan*, 'drawn'; likewise, OI. *kiōsa*, OE. *cēosan*, OS. *keosan*, and OHG. *kiosan*, 'to choose,' but OI. *kørenn*, OE. *coren*, and OS. and OHG. *gi-koran*, 'chosen.'

There were in Indo-European types of nouns in which the position of the accent varied with the inflection. This variation is clearly preserved in Lithuanian, where one finds, for example, acc. sg. *ākmeni*, 'stone,' but gen. sg. *akmeñs*; acc. sg. *gálvą*, 'head,' but gen. sg. *galvōs*; acc. sg. *sūnų*, 'son,' but gen. sg. *sūnaũs*. These alternations undoubtedly explain oppositions in the forms of nouns in the Germanic dialects, such as Got. *auso* (gen. *ausins*), 'ear,' but OI. *eyra*, OE. *ēare*, and OHG. *ōra*; or Got. *dauþs*, 'death,' but OS. *dōd* and OHG. *tōt*. Examples of this sort are numerous.

Therefore, at the date when **s* and the spirants placed between two voiced elements became voiced, the Indo-European accent, of which there is no longer a trace in Germanic of the historic epoch, still existed, and the presence of this accent on the initial syllable of the word sufficed to prevent the voicing of a sibilant or of a spirant which immediately followed it.

Verner's Law is proved only for the spirant which follows the vocalic cut of the initial syllable of the word.

In the rest of the word, the ancient voiceless spirants are also represented, sometimes by voiceless consonants and at other times by voiced consonants. In Gothic the distribution is regulated by dissimilation: the sibilants and spirants between voiced phonemes become voiced if the preceding syllable begins with a voiceless phoneme; they remain (or become again?) voiceless if the preceding syllable begins with a voiced phoneme. Hence we have *aupida*, 'desert,' but *meripa*, 'noise'; or *witubni*, 'science,' but *waldufni*, 'power.' For the other dialects, in the same situation, the principle of the distribution of voiceless and voiced spirants is unknown.

The voicing of sibilants and spirants placed between voiced sounds is an act of assimilation to the neighboring phonemes. An initial consonant is in a less critical position than an interior consonant, but assimilation is also conceivable in this situation; initial *s* has become voiced in German: *so* is pronounced *zo*. In some instances, the initial spirants of English dialects become voiced; thus *þ* becomes *d*. All English shows this phenomenon in accessory words: *th* initial is normally voiceless in English, unlike *th* intervocalic, which is voiced; but the article *the* has a voiced *th*. A similar development occurred in the case of the unaccented personal pronouns from a prehistoric date in several dialects. Parallel to Lat. *tu*, 'you,' we find as principal accented forms Got. *þu*, OI. *þū*, OS. *thū*, and OHG. *dū*, but there is an accessory form, unaccented, which has become *du*, found in Old Icelandic -*du* (-*do*) and in Old High German -*tu*: *nimis-tu*, 'you take' (modern Ger. *nimmst*). The action of vowels tending to voice sibilants and spirants extends then very far in Germanic.

However, what has had a decisive influence on the development of the language is the fact that the alteration of intervocalic consonants never reached the point of suppression. What makes Latin words unrecognizable in the forms they have taken in French is that intervocalic consonants have been radically altered or even reduced to the point of disappearance; in Fr. *feu* we no longer recognize Latin *focum*; in *père* we no longer recognize Latin *patrem*; in *mi*, we no longer recognize Latin *medium*. In Germanic nothing like this has happened. Certain consonants have changed aspect, but they have persisted; others, like the Germanic voiceless *p, *t*, and *k*, are stable in most dialects. In short, the words have kept intact the separation between syllables which is made by the consonants and which forms, so to speak, the skeleton of the words. From an ancient *kápiti, 'he takes,' we get Got. *hafjiþ* (replacing *hafiþ) and OHG. *hevit*. The consonants are not so well preserved as in the corresponding Lat. *capit*, but the overall structure is the same. *Vater* and *Mitte* are closer in appearance to Lat. *patrem* and *medium* than are Fr. *père* and *mi*. Thus it is that Indo-European words are often recognizable in Germanic down to the present in spite of the number and seriousness of the intervening phonetic changes.

A marked alteration of intervocalic consonants is one of the characteristic traits of Celtic languages—under different forms in Gaelic and Breton. French has inherited this Celtic tendency, and we have just seen that Germanic shows a similar but less powerful tendency.

Chapter III

The Vocalic System

WE MUST distinguish in Indo-European the true vowels, which show only three qualities, *a, e, and o, and the sonants. The latter function sometimes as consonants before a vowel—*y, w, r, l, m, and n; sometimes as vowels before a consonant or at the end of a word—*i, u, ṛ, ḷ, ṃ, and ṇ; and sometimes after a true vowel and before a consonant or at the end of a word as second elements of diphthongs—for example, *ei, eu, er, el, en, and em.

The true vowels were either short or long; they can therefore be distinguished as *e, ē, o, ō, a, and ā. In Indo-European still another vocalic element was distinguished which we designate by the sign *ə; in the initial syllable of a word, this *ə is confused with short *a in Germanic, as it is in most Indo-European languages except Indo-Iranian where *ə is represented by *i. In interior syllables, *ə ordinarily disappears in Germanic, as it does in Iranian, Armenian, Slavic, and Baltic; or, if it is represented by some vowel in cases difficult to determine, it is by one of the Germanic vowels, *a, i, or u. Practically, we have to consider only *e, o, and a, short and long.

This vocalic system, already limited in variety, was further reduced in Germanic: the qualities o and a were confused. A similar confusion took place also in Baltic, Slavic, and Albanian; Indo-Iranian, which merges the three qualities a, e, and o into a, has gone still farther. The distinction between o and a was maintained in Greek, Italic, Celtic, and Armenian; there are traces in Letto-Lithuanian only for the long vowels.

To the two short vowels o and a of Greek, Italic, Celtic, and Armenian, Germanic corresponds with the single vowel *a. We have then a in Got. akrs, 'field,' OI. akr, and OHG. achar, opposite the a of Skr. ájraḥ, Gr. agrós, Lat. ager, and Arm. art (with altered consonant). The same is true in Got. fadar, 'father,' OI. fader, and OHG. fater, opposite Lat. pater, Gr. patḗr, OIr. athir, Arm. hayr, and Skr. pitá (with i showing that it is a question of ancient *ə). Likewise we have a in Got. ahtau, 'eight,' OI. átta, and OHG. ahto, opposite the o of Lat. octō, Gr. októ, OIr. ocht; also we find Got. asts, 'branch,' and OHG. ast, opposite Gr. ózdos and Arm. ost.

To the two long vowels *ā* and *ō* of Greek and Italic, which are also distinguished in Celtic and Armenian, Germanic corresponds with long **o*; the long vowels are then represented by a more closed vowel than the one which represents the corresponding short vowels. Thus we have Got. *broþar*, 'brother,' OI. *brōþer*, OS. *brōther*, and OHG. *bruoder*, opposite Lat. *frāter* and Gr. *phrātōr*, just as we have Got. *bloma*, 'flower,' OI. *blōme*, OS. *blōmo*, and OHG. *bluomo*, opposite Lat. *flōs*.

As for the system of sonants, it is dislocated by the fact that the functioning of the three types—consonant, vowel, and second element of a diphthong—is not maintained.

The sonant consonants **y, w, r, l, m,* and *n* are maintained without notable change in common Germanic and do not call for comment. The loss of *y* and *w* at the beginning of words under certain conditions is a peculiarity characteristic of Nordic.

The sonant vowels change character. The two most vocalic, *i* and *u*, are considered as true vowels with short and long forms. The four others, **r̥, l̥, n̥,* and *m̥*, are replaced by diphthongs in *u*: **ur, ul, un,* and *um*. Take, for example, **r̥* in one of the words for which the root is **ters-*, 'to dry,' Skr. *tr̥ṣúḥ*, 'thirsty, eager'; corresponding to it we find Got. *þaursus*, 'dry,' OI. *þurr*, and OHG. *durri* (the *s* interior of Got. *þaursus*, instead of the expected *z*, is analogous to *-þairsan*, 'to dry'). For **m̥* in the first syllable, corresponding to Skr. *çatám*, 'hundred,' Gr. *-katón*, Lat. *centum*, and Lit. *šimtas*, we find Got. *hund* and OHG. *hunt* (**m* became **n* in Germanic before a dental occlusive).

When sonants were found between a consonant and a vowel, they could be broken in Indo-European into a very short vowel followed by a sonant consonant. The very short vowel had qualities which varied in the different Indo-European dialects. Greek, for example, had *ar, al, an,* and *am* in such cases. Germanic had **u* in **ur, ul, un,* and *um*, as for example in Got. *sums*, 'someone' (from **sumaz*), and OS. and OHG. *sum*, opposite Gr. *hamo-* (in *oud-amos*, 'nobody'); or as in Got. *faura*, 'in front of,' OE. *for*, and OHG. *fora* (with *o* issuing from *u* in all dialects), opposite Skr. *purá*, 'before,' and Gr. *para*.

The Indo-European diphthongs formed three series in *e, o,* and *a*—thus **ei, oi,* and *ai* or **en, on,* and *an*, for example. As a result of the merging of *o* and of *a*, these three series were reduced to two in Germanic; we have Got. *ains* and OI. *einn*, 'one,' opposite OLat. *oinos* and Gr. *oino-*, and Got. *ais*, 'bronze,' and OI. *eir*, opposite Lat. *aes*.

In all the Indo-European languages, the diphthongs tend to become simplified, and this often happens rather early. In Sanskrit the simplification of **ai* and **au* to long *e* and *o* had already taken place at the time of

32 General Characteristics of the Germanic Languages

the oldest texts. In Germanic, on the contrary, the diphthongs have been very resistant. Only the diphthong *ei, the two elements of which are phonetically very close to one another, was simplified to i prior to the time of the oldest texts in all the dialects. The Germanic diphthongs *ai and au are still diphthongs today in German except for certain special cases. All the simplifications of diphthongs which have taken place have been produced independently in each of the Germanic dialects; and the diversity of treatment of the diphthongs in the various dialects has a lot to do with the different aspects presented by the same words from one Germanic language to another.

In accordance with the preceding statements, we expect to find in Germanic the following system: short vowels—*a, e, i, and u,—and long vowels—*ō, ē, ī, and ū,—to which must be added the diphthongs ai, au, an, am, ar, al, and so forth. This is indeed approximately what we find.

Common Germanic *ē, representing an ancient ē, is represented in Gothic by e (that is to say long close e) and in Nordic and in the Western dialects by ā (at least in the initial syllable; by ē in the other syllables). Thus we have Got. sēþs, 'seed,' OI. sād, OE. sǣed, OS. sād, and OHG. sāt, opposite Lat. sē-men. There is another *ē of obscure origin—and surely of various origins—which has a special treatment in Scandinavian and in the Western dialects; for example, we have Got. hēr, 'here,' opposite OI., OE., and OS. hēr (with ē and not ā), and OHG. hear, hiar.

All the ancient short *e's are not represented in the various Germanic dialects by e, nor are all the short *i's represented by i; in reality the i's and the e's of the different dialects correspond to ancient *i or *e almost indifferently, and the distribution of i and e is defined by rules peculiar to each of the Germanic dialects. Everything has happened then almost as if there had been in common Germanic a single vowel, which became i or e according to the cases. Moreover, in the conditions where e appears in each dialect, we observe that ancient *u is ordinarily represented by short o, which does not correspond to an ancient Indo-European *ŏ, but is a Germanic creation. Thus we find ourselves far from the Indo-European system.

This is because a radically new principle has intervened. Each vowel of the Indo-European word has its autonomy, and the vocalic element of the syllable does not depend to any degree on the neighboring consonants or vowels. In Germanic, on the contrary, the quality of the vowels, in the first place of short vowels and later even of long vowels, is ordered by their place in the word and by the consonant and vowel elements which follow them in the same word.

This principle had only just begun in common Germanic, but we find applications of it in all the Germanic dialects, and the effects are all the more marked when we observe a more advanced period of the history of a given dialect. The actions of the consonants and vowels on the preceding vowels were produced or at least completed for the most part during the historical period. Inasmuch as they took place independently in each dialect, the vowel system has taken on different aspects in the various Germanic dialects. The English, Danish, Swedish, and German vowel systems are now quite distinct from one another.

The Gothic vowel system, in its extreme simplicity, is instructive with regard to the common Germanic type. It includes three short vowels, *a*, *i*, and *u*, and four long vowels, *ō*, *ē*, *i*, and *ū*. The vowels *e* and *o* are close; since they are always long, we do not indicate the quantity. The vowel *i* is written *ei*. The vowel *ū* does not have a notation different from that of *ŭ*. The short vowels *i* and *u* take the qualities of open *e* and *o* before the consonants *h* and *r*; they are then written *ai* and *au*. For example, opposite OS. *tugun* and OHG. *zugun*, 'they drew,' Gothic has *tauhun* (with *h* replacing *g* from the singular *tauh* and the present *tiuhan*). Before *r* and *h* Gothic then has *ĕ* (written *ai*), whether it had earlier been *e* or *i*; thus we have Got. *wair*, 'man,' opposite Lat. *uir*, and *faihu*, 'money' (originally 'herd'), opposite Lat. *pecu*, 'herd.' With the distribution of *i* and *u* and of *ĕ* and *ŏ* being thus regulated by a constant formula, Gothic teaches us nothing about the treatment of *i, *e*, and *u* in common Germanic. However, from this treatment it is brought out on the one hand that *i and *ĕ tended to become confused, and on the other that *i and *ŭ were subject to the influence of a following consonant.

To judge from Nordic and West Germanic, ancient *e became *i at an early date, undoubtedly in common Germanic, before a nasal: to OIr. *sēt* (from *sent) and Middle Breton *hent*, 'road,' Germanic corresponds with Got. *sinþs*, OI. *sinn*, OE. *sid* (from *sinþ), and OHG. *sind*. The *i thus produced has always remained *i*, just as *u before a nasal has always remained *u*.

It appears that in any unaccented syllable (see the following chapter on accent), *e has changed to *i; but this cannot easily be illustrated with clear examples.

In West Germanic and less clearly in Nordic, the distribution of *e* and *o*, on the one hand, and of *i* and *u*, on the other, in the initial syllable of the word, is regulated by a simple formula: we have *e* or *o* if the following syllable has *a* or *ō*, and we have *i* or *u* if the following syllable has a vowel of the quality of *i* or *u* or if there is a *y* consonant. A word like *wiros, 'man' (cf. Lat. *uir*) will give us *wiraz, from which we have OI. *verr* and OE.,

OS., and OHG. *wer* with *e*; from **bheronon*, 'action of carrying,' we get the infinitive OI. *bera*, and OE., OS., and OHG. *beran*, 'to carry.' However, it is sufficient to introduce *i* or *u* for *i* to appear at least dialectally: OHG. *biru*, 'I carry' (from **bherō*; on *ō* final, see p. 47), *biris*, 'you carry' (from **bheresi*), *birit*, 'he carries' (cf. OR. *beretĭ*), opposite *beramēs*, 'we carry' (cf. Gr. *phéromen*, with a little different ending), and *berant*, 'they carry' (cf. Dorian Gr. *phéronti*). Old High German likewise opposes *erda*, 'earth' (cf. Gr. *érazde*, 'on the earth') to *irdīn*, 'of earth.' Before **-dhy-*, **e* also becomes *i* in all German dialects: Skr. *mádhyaḥ*, 'which is in the middle.' and Lat. *medius*, as opposed to OI. *midr*, OE. *midd*, and OHG. *mitti*.

Likewise *u* is maintained before *i* and *u*; thus **sunuz*, 'son' (cf. Skr. *sūnúḥ* and Lit. *sūnùs*), gives old runic Norse *sunuR*, and OE., OS., and OHG. *sunu*; but a common Germanic **yukan* (cf. Skr. *yugám*, Gr. *zdygón*, and Lat. *iugum*), 'yoke,' gives OI. *ok*, OE. *geoc*, and OHG. *joh*, opposite Got. *juk*. These facts are moreover disturbed by a multiplicity of analogous actions and special influences.

There has been speculation as to whether the transformation of *ŭ* to *ŏ* before a syllable containing *a* or *ō* occurred in Gothic and whether Gothic again confused the two vowels in its *u*. The name of the Goths is *Gutones* in Strabo and Pliny, *Gotones* in Tacitus. However the form with *o* found in Tacitus and found again thereafter may have been borrowed from other Germanic dialects; it does not necessarily reproduce a Gothic pronunciation. Moreover, the Gothic of Ulfila does not provide sufficient evidence that the pronunciation *u* was universal in Gothic. The problem is unsettled for lack of data.

The general agreement between Nordic and West Germanic guarantees that the passage of **i* (representing **e* and **i*) and of **u* to **e* and **o* before a syllable containing *a* or *ō* is of great antiquity, and the written forms *Gotones* of Tacitus and *Gothi* of Trebellius Pollio attest that from the beginning of the Christian era the *o* existed in a part of Germanic, notably among the Goths. The passage of **e* to **i* under the influence of an **i* in a following syllable was not yet completed in common Nordic, for one reads in runic Norse *erilaR* (the word *iarl* of Old Icelandic), which is all the more reason why it cannot pass for common Germanic. However, the agreement of Nordic with the group of Western dialects shows that the tendency at least is common Germanic.

The vowel *i* and the consonant *j* have continued to act after having occasioned the changes we have just seen. In Nordic and West Germanic these elements tend to transform **a* to *e* under conditions which vary from dialect to dialect; sometimes the results agree, sometimes they do not agree. For example, opposite Got. *satjan*, 'to seat,' we have OI. *setia*, OE.

settan, OS. *settian*, and OHG. *sezzen*, everywhere with *e*. But from **gastiz*, 'guest,' which is *-gastiR* in the oldest Norse runic texts, we have from A.D. 700 *-gestr* and OI. *gestr*; likewise Old English has *giest*, while Old Saxon and Old High German have *gast*; on the other hand, in the plural before preserved *i*, Old Saxon and Old High German have *gesti* (cf. Got. *gasteis*). The details of these actions belong to the individual study of each Germanic dialect.

The alteration of *u* by a following *i* developed late in the German dialects; it is not yet noted in the Old High German texts. Let us take for example the common Germanic **fullaz*, 'full,' attested by Got. *fulls* (cf. OSl. *plŭnŭ*, Lit. *pìlnas*, and, with a special treatment of **ḷ* which we have no occasion to examine here, Skr. *pūrṇáh*); the *u* of **ul* normally became *o* in OHG. *fol* (*follēr*), while under the influence of other forms it remained *u* in OE. and OS. *full*; to the derived Got. verb *fulljan*, 'to fill,' correspond OI. *fylla* and OE. *fyllan*, while Old High German has *fullen*; nevertheless the *u* has also been inflected in German; the alteration is noted already in Middle High German, and modern High German has *ü* in *füllen*, just as English has *i* in *fill*.

The long vowels, at first spared, have been strongly affected in their turn in Old English and in Nordic; for example to Got. *sokjan*, 'to seek' (cf. Lat. *sāgiō*), corresponds OHG. *suohhen*, without alteration; but we have OI. *søkia* and OE. *sēcan* (modern English *seek*).

The very complex ensemble of the alterations of vowels under the influence of following *i, j*, and *u* is known in German under the name *Umlaut*. We may call it in French *inflexion* (the term *métaphonie* has also been proposed).

The "*inflexion*" is not the only change the vowels have undergone under the influence of neighboring phonemes. Consonants also act upon them. For example, in German where the diphthongs *ai* and *au* are maintained as a general rule, these same diphthongs are simplified to *e* and *o* before *h* and *r*: Got. *air*, 'sooner,' OHG. *er*; Got. *hauhs*, 'high,' OHG. *hoh*; and so on. In English the short vowels are broken before *r*: to Got. *wairþan*, 'to throw,' and OHG. *werfan*, Old English corresponds with *weorþan*; to Got. *arm*, 'arm,' and OHG. *arm*, Old English corresponds with *earm*; and so forth.

In Nordic it is the vowels of the following syllables which bring about the "breaking" of short vowels. Thus *e* breaks into *ea* or *ia* before *a* in the following syllable: **ebnaz* (Got. *ibns*, OHG. *eban*) becomes OI. *iafn*, OSw. *iamm*; *e* breaks into *eo* or *io* before **u* in the following syllable: we have OI. and OSw. *miolk*, opposite Got. *miluks*, 'milk,' and OFr. *melok*.

Only a detailed study of each of the Germanic dialects at every epoch and almost in each of its local varieties would determine all these delicate and infinitely varied actions. The Germanic vowel system, at first simple, has become progressively more complicated and has acquired all sorts of new types, delicately distinguished, especially in English and the Scandinavian languages.

Like the principle of the mutation of the occlusives and the alteration of intervocalic consonants, the tendency of vowels to conform to the articulation of neighboring phonemes is found also in Celtic: in Irish as in Germanic, for example, it is impossible in general to determine whether an *e* or an *i* is based on an ancient *e* or on an ancient *i*.

Chapter IV

The Initial Accent of Intensity

THE INDO-EUROPEAN "accent" consisted of an elevation of the voice bearing on one of the syllables of the word. It was a pitch accent. We have proof of it, first from the descriptions which the Indians gave of the Vedic accent and from those given by the Greeks of the accent of ancient Greek, and, second, from the fact that the accent had no effect on the quality and the quantity of the vowels during the ancient period. In a general way, the tonic and the atonic vowels are treated alike in all the ancient forms of the languages in which the Indo-European pitch accent was maintained down to historic times: in Sanskrit, Greek, Slavic, and Baltic. Nowhere do we see that the Indo-European "tone" exerted any influence on the pronunciation of the vowels between the Indo-European period and that of the most ancient monuments of each language.

The pitch accent could occur anywhere in the Indo-European word. The position of the pitch was not determined by phonetic conditions; it served to characterize the word and the grammatical forms. For example, a singular like Skr. *émi,* 'I go,' has the accent on the initial vowel, while a plural like Skr. *imáḥ,* 'we go,' has the accent on the final vowel.

Verner's Law, explained in Chapter II, shows that the Indo-European pitch accent still existed in Germanic at the time when the consonant mutation was completed. It has since disappeared. Naturally we cannot affirm that no trace of it remained at the time of the appearance of the most ancient texts, the first runic inscriptions, or at the time of the translation of the Bible into Gothic in the fourth century. However, nowhere at a historic date is there anything which indicates a preservation of the pitch accent in Germanic.

The Indo-European pitch did not intervene in the rhythm of the language. The versification of Sanskrit, ancient Greek, and Latin, as well as the rhythmic prose of Greek and Latin, is based only on the alternation of long and short syllables. Pitch was not tied to quantity in Indo-European; it was linked to quantity only in a secondary and partial way in Greek and Latin. The opposition of long and short vowels was maintained in a firm manner in all the ancient Indo-European languages. Except in the finals, where there have been some losses in a well-defined case, Lithuanian preserves even today the opposition of long and short vowels; also except for finals, Serbian and Czech show important traces of this contrast.

The opposition of long and short vowels persisted in common Germanic; alterations of the quantity of syllables in common Germanic occur only in the final syllable. Except in the final syllable, Gothic displays, completely preserved, all the oppositions between long and short vowels. However, if we go from there to the most ancient texts of Nordic or West Germanic dialects, we perceive that many of the long vowels have been shortened; except for the initial syllable, the quantity and often the quality of the vowels have been profoundly disturbed.

So it is that here again a decisive change has intervened in common Germanic.

The initial syllable of every principal word in the sentence received an accent of intensity. This accent, exemplified in present-day German and English in all its force, exercised a considerable action. It maintained the long vowels on which it fell, tending even to lengthen the short syllables by lengthening either the vowel of the syllable or the consonant element by which it was separated from the second syllable of the word. It tended to shorten the long vowels in the unaccented syllables.

The rhythm of the language since then has depended only on this accent. Germanic versification is based on the alternation of accented and unaccented syllables. The special importance of the initial syllables in the versification of the ancient Germanic dialects is marked in addition by the important role that the alliterations of the initial consonants play.

The Germanic sentence is hammered out by the accents of intensity which strike the initial syllables of each of the principal words.

Long words receive also a secondary accent, the study of which belongs to the examination of each particular dialect.

The introduction of the accent of intensity at a fixed place was a revolution, and there is nothing which is more distinctive about Germanic.

The existence of a very strong accent of intensity, to which everything else in the language is subordinated, is not frequent. Most Indo-European languages and, outside of Indo-European, most of the languages of the world have nothing like it. We find an accent of intensity in other languages besides Germanic, but almost nowhere do we find an accent so strong and active. Accustomed by their language to see in the accent the principal agent of phonetic changes, German linguists have often exaggerated the role of the accent in the languages which they were studying. In the modern languages of Europe in which the sing-song element is being attenuated, the accent plays a notable role; but except in Russian it has almost nowhere an importance comparable to that which we see in the West Germanic languages.

Of course, Germanic is not the only Indo-European language which has an accent of intensity, nor is it the only one which has fixed the accent at a certain place in the word. Features comparable to these features of Germanic may be observed in neighboring Western languages. In Celtic, Irish also fixed an accent of intensity on the initial syllable of the word, an accent equally strong producing actions equally important; but the other Celtic dialects do not have an accent on the initial syllable, and, if the Brythonic dialects have an accent of intensity, this accent does not have the force of that of Germanic. In very ancient Latin, the initial syllable of words was not treated like the other syllables. The short syllables of the interior syllables were subjected to very serious alterations which the initial syllables escaped; but the particular pronunciation of the initial syllable was eliminated by the time of the beginning of the historic period. The closest of the neighboring dialects, Oscan and Umbrian, did not alter the vowels in the same manner. In Germanic, on the contrary, the accent on the initial vowel is a feature of the entire group, and it has a singular force which has manifested its effects during the whole historical development of this group.

In the Gothic of Ulfila, as has been noted, the effects of the initial accent are almost invisible. At the most, there are only a few words which allow us to suspect its existence.

However, the agreement of the Nordic and West Germanic dialects precludes any doubt that the initial accent of intensity tended to become established from the time of common Germanic.

Like the consonant mutation and the profound transformation of the vowel system, this fact suggests an outside influence. Here is a type of pronunciation foreign to Indo-European; it was introduced by the population which learned to speak the dialect which has become Germanic.

From the moment it was introduced, this accent was imposed on the whole language. Borrowed words did not escape. When Latin words were borrowed, these received the initial accent; and thus it is that the Latin *aséllus*, accented on -*sel*-, became *asilus* (Gothic form), accented on the *a*-, and that we have OHG. *esil* and modern Ger. *esel*, while the Slavic has kept the accent of the Latin word in *osĭlŭ*, which has become *osël* in Russian, with the accent on -*sel*. The Latin word *palátium*, accented on

-la-, has given us in French *palais*, but in German it is *pfalz* because of the accent on the initial syllable. It is only with time, under the influence of compound Germanic formations in which the accent was fixed on a non-initial element (German type *erfinden* or *empfángen*, for example), that the speakers of Germanic learned again to put the accent on a syllable other than the initial one and that foreign words were borrowed with the accent remaining on a noninitial syllable.

The action of the initial accent on the vowel system has been consider-able. The accent has acted upon the quantity and the quality of the vowels.

In the initial syllable, the opposition of long and short vowels was maintained at first in an exact manner, while in unaccented syllables the long vowels tended to become short and the short to disappear. With time, the short vowels in an open accented syllable tended to become long; for example, the ancient short *e* of a word like OHG. *geban* has become long in the modern German *geben*.

The difference in treatment of long accented syllables and long un-accented syllables is striking: accented *ē* became *ā* during the first centuries of the Christian era in Scandinavian and West Germanic, so that the ancient name *Suēbi*, which we read in Caesar and which the Greeks write Σουῆβοι, has changed to *Swāb*. In the second syllable, however, the *ē* of verbs in -*ē*- persists, and we have OHG. *habēmēs*, 'we have.' In Old High German the long vowels of unaccented syllables remain, and it is only during the Middle Ages that these long vowels were shortened; in Scandinavian the shortening of long unaccented vowels is characteristic of common Nordic. For example, from the common Germanic word **gulþan*, represented by Got. *gulþ*, OI. *gull*, and OHG. *gold*, we get the derived Got. *gulþeins*, 'of gold,' and OHG. *guldīn* with *i*, but OI. *gullenn*.

In more or less remote antiquity, the entire system, so fundamental to Indo-European, of the opposition of long syllables and short syllables was overthrown. By eliminating it, moreover, Germanic has only done what has been done at various dates in most Indo-European languages: the delicate opposition of long and short vowels has had a tendency to dis-appear, and only a small number of Indo-European languages, notably Lithuanian and Serbian, present it today more or less completely.

The disappearance of short interior unaccented vowels is a characteristic trait of Germanic. In the beginning, this disappearance depended on the quantity of the preceding accented syllable. What illustrates the per-sistence of the Indo-European importance of long syllables is that a short vowel disappears sooner after a long syllable than it does after a short syllable. Thus in the preterites called "weak," Old High German opposes the form with *i* of the type in *zelita* (infinitive *zellen*, 'to count'; cf. OS. *tellian*, from *taljan) to the form without *i* of the type *suohta* (cf. Got. *sokida*; infinitive OHG. *suohhen*, 'to seek,' from *sōkjan); similarly, we have *nerita*, 'he cured,' but *hōrta*, 'he heard,' and so on. We observe analogous phenomena in Old English and in Scandinavian, but in each language the manner is independent and follows rules of detail peculiar to each.

What especially characterizes Germanic is the way in which it has altered the quality of unaccented vowels. In general, the ancient forms of Nordic and West Germanic still show *a*, *i*, and *u* distinctly, even for short vowels of unaccented syllables. Then the short unaccented vowels tended to be reduced to a single, banal quality which is represented as *e*. The alteration appears first in the preverbs, particles which are welded to the verbs and which are found consequently in the syllable which immediately precedes the accented syllable. Like Gothic, the most ancient Old High German in the eighth century still has *ga-*; then this *ga-* changes to *ge-*, which becomes *gi-* toward the ninth century; later *ge-* is uniformly used, beginning with the last period of Old High German; hence we have *ga-zogan*, *gi-zogan*, *ge-zogan*. Likewise *fur-* and *for-* of the most ancient Old High German become *fir-*, then *fer-*. Thus it is with all the ancient preverbs. In German and in English the unaccented vowels progressively lost their particular qualities. The quality of unaccented vowels has been better preserved in the Scandinavian languages, in spite of numerous alterations, because the accent is much less intense in these languages than in German and English.

The initial accent of intensity has not exerted much influence on the treatment of consonants. There is a common Germanic innovation which we might be tempted to attribute to the presence of the initial accent of intensity: it is the gemination of *y and *w in a certain number of cases. Thus opposite genitive Skr. *dváyoḥ*, 'of two,' and OSl. *dvoju*, we find OHG. *zweiio* (*zweio*), OS. *tweio*, OI. *tueggia*, and Got. *twaddje*, all forms which imply geminate *y*. An ancient *triwaz, 'faithful,' becomes *triuwaz in OS. and OHG. *triuwi*, OE. *trēowe*, OI. *tryggr*, and Got. *triggws*. However, in reality it is a question of an expressive gemination inherited from Indo-European, whose fortune has been unusually good in Germanic. The type OHG. *zweiio* should be compared with Gr. *doios*, 'double,' ancient *dwoiyós, that is, *dwoyyos. The type OHG. *triuwi* is comparable to the Lat. type *lippus*. Germanic has many verbs like OHG. *lecchōn*, opposite the Lat. *ligūriō* (it will be noticed that in such a case the ancient voiceless and ancient voiced aspirated consonants become voiceless in Germanic like the simple ancient voiced consonants).

Besides Germanic, the only group in which the accent of intensity has had such great importance is Celtic. In Irish the initial accent of intensity has produced results similar to those produced by the German or English accent.

Chapter V

Treatment of Word Endings

THE TREATMENT of the endings of polysyllabic words must be distinguished from the general treatment of unaccented syllables. The final syllable of polysyllabic words participates in the general weakness of unaccented syllables in Germanic. However, it has a special weakness which belongs to its final character: the alterations which take place in all unaccented syllables were produced earlier and more completely in the final syllable of the word than in the interior. The special character of the finals dates from Indo-European, and in all the languages of the group the special consequences of this position are apparent, even where there is no accent of intensity and where all the other syllables of the word have a single and same treatment of the same phonetic elements.

The treatment of finals is imperfectly understood. Examples of each type of fact are rare, and the original Indo-European is not always determinable. We work with grammatical forms that are suspect by their very nature of having undergone analogous actions.

Moreover, word endings are subject to varied influences. The end of the word is found in different positions: at a pause, before a word with which the word is linked, before a word with which there is no linking, before a vowel, or before a consonant. In addition, the treatment can also vary according to the character of the following consonant. Sanskrit, in which the end of the word is written in various fashions depending on the initial phoneme of the following word, gives us an idea of this variety. Finally, the treatment is not necessarily the same for the same word in all cases, for the importance of the word is not always the same in the sentence. If the word has a dominant role, it is pronounced more slowly and more distinctly; if it has an accessory role, it is pronounced more quickly and with less care. These differences are manifested particularly in finals because the final position, naturally weak, makes the elements of which it is composed susceptible to all influences. To combat a variety of forms for the final of the same word the language is led to react; for the same word, for the same grammatical type, it tends to choose one of the forms, often the one which is the best adapted phonetically to the majority of situations. The phonetic type chosen is not necessarily the same in all words. We must not then expect to find in word endings phonetic correspondences as regular as those we observe in the rest of the word.

Consequently, we shall indicate only general tendencies which can be recognized, and we shall abstain from laying down absolute rules which might turn out to be false.

Final consonants were not uttered with an explosion in Indo-European; they were reduced to an implosion by which the vowel of the final syllable is arrested. As a result, these consonants have tended to disappear; whenever they have not been eliminated, they often show special treatment.

The only occlusive on which we have data is the dental occlusive. Like the Italic dialects, Germanic has known only one sort of final dental. In monosyllables where the occlusive has been maintained, this dental is a voiceless *-t, which, following the rules of mutation, represents an ancient *-d. Opposite the nominative-accusative singular neuter Skr. *tát* (*tád* before a voiced phoneme), 'this,' and Lat. *is-tud*, we have then OI. *þat*, OS. *that*, and OHG. *daz*; Gothic has *þat-a*, with the addition of a particle *-a*. Likewise, to Lat. *quod*, 'what,' corresponds OI. *huat*, OS. *(h)wat*, and OHG. *(h)waz*. A final dental in a polysyllable disappears in all dialects; opposite Skr. *bháret*, 'may he carry,' we have Got. *bairai*, 'let him carry,' OI. *bere*, and OHG. *bere*.

The sibilant -s (-z) is frequent at the end of words in Indo-European. All the evidence agrees that common Germanic represented the final Indo-European sibilant by the voiced *-z. Gothic, which made final spirants voiceless, has -s instead of -z; the -z persists only in a few cases where there is a following particle, closely linked in pronunciation, and where the z, treated as in the interior of the word, has therefore been maintained. Nordic made of final *-z an -r. In the runic alphabet this is written with a special sign, distinct from that which indicates an ancient r; the usual transcription is R. In Old Icelandic there is the ordinary r. In West Germanic the final *-z has disappeared in all the polysyllables, and it has remained in monosyllables only in the form -r. A nominative-singular IE. *ghostis (cf. Lat. *hostis*, 'foreigner, enemy') became in Gothic *gasts*, 'guest,' runic Old Norse -*gastiR*, OI. *gestr*, OE. *giest*, and OHG. *gast*. For the conservation of -z in Gothic and of -r in Old High German, we can cite forms of the indefinite interrogative and of the demonstratives: opposite Lit. *kàs* and Skr. *káḥ*, Gothic has *hwas*, 'who' (*hwaz*- in *hwaz-uh*, 'each one'), and opposite Lat. *quis* and ancient Iranian *čiš*, Old High German has *(h)wer*; opposite Lat. *is*, Gothic has *is* (and *iz*- in *iz-ei*, 'who' relative), and Old High German has *er*. The *r* of OHG. (*h*)*wer* and *er* persisted in German in the form *thēr*, from which we have *der*, which serves as a nominative for the demonstrative *tha-*, corresponding to Got. *þa-* (cf. Skr. *tá-*) and the "strong" inflection of masculine adjectives.

The final nasal appears in Indo-Iranian and Italic with the form -*m*, in the other languages with the form -*n*. This nasal is maintained in Germanic only in monosyllables after a short vowel. We find, for example, Got. *hwan*, 'when,' opposite Lat. *quom*, and Got. *þan*, 'then,' opposite Lat. *tum*; in the accusative masculine singular we have opposite Skr. *tám*, 'this one,' OI. *þan*, OS. *than*, and OHG *den* (with an analogic change of vowel), and, with the addition of a particle, Got. *þan-a*, OE. *don-e*, and OS. *than-a*. In polysyllables the final nasal disappears; thus for the nominative-accusative neuter singulars for which the final is Skr. -*am*, Lat. -*um*, Gr. -*on*, and OPr. -*an*, we find -*a* in old runic Norse—for example, *horna*, 'horn.'

The changes to which vowels in final syllables were subjected were of greater consequence than those which affected consonants. These vowels tended to undergo a shortening, which caused the short vowels to disappear and the long ones to become short. That being the case, final syllables tending to lose their vowels either ceased to exist or were reduced, and the whole general aspect of the word was changed. The tendency to shorten the vowels of final syllables is not peculiar to Germanic; it is manifested also for example in common Slavic, Lithuanian, and Latin. In Germanic this natural tendency has been augmented by the intensity of the initial syllables. The destruction of the vowels of final syllables began early and has never ceased, so that the development of Germanic is dominated by this progressive elimination, which continues still today.

In common Germanic there is reason to believe that the short vowels of final syllables remained intact. Nevertheless, no text, not even the most ancient runic inscriptions, has kept an *a* or *i* final. Thus in the preterite, where the first-person singular was in **-a* (Gr. *oida*, 'I know') and the third was in **-e* (Gr. *oide*, 'he knows'), old runic Norse already has *nam*, 'I took,' which has lost an **-a* final, and *gaf*, 'he gave,' which has lost an **-i* final (ancient **-e*); the final **-eti* of the present tense of verbs is already -*iþ* in old runic Norse, as in Gothic.

Insofar as forms are attested, old runic Norse keeps nearly all short vowels in final syllables where the vowel was followed by a consonant. For example, before -*R* representing **-z* final (ancient **-s*), we regularly find -*aR*, -*iR*, and -*uR*; the final nasal -*n* has disappeared, but the preceding vowel has been maintained: -*a*, -*i*, and -*u* represent **-an*, **-in*, and **-un*.

However, from the beginning of the eighth century, we find simply -*R* instead of ancient -*aR* or -*iR*.

In Gothic, the disappearance of short -*a* and *i* dates back farther. Corresponding to old runic Norse *stainaR*, Gothic has *stains*; to old runic Norse -*gastiR*, it has *gasts*. On the contrary, *-uz* is regularly maintained in the form -*us*, as in *sunus*, 'son.' Ancient *-an* and *-in*, maintained in old runic Norse in the forms -*a* and -*i*, have disappeared in Gothic where we find *stain* and *gast* opposite old runic Norse *staina* and *gasti* in the masculine accusative singular; on the other hand, we have Got. *sunu*, in which the vowel -*u* is maintained. Even the *u* of an absolute final persists: Got. *filu*, 'much,' with *u* which is preserved also in OE. *feolu* and OHG. *filu* (from **pelu*), opposite neuter Gr. *polú*, 'much.'

As for West Germanic, the ancient *-az* and *-an*, and *-iz* and *-in* have been reduced to zero since the earliest tradition, and we find OE. *stān* and *giest*, and OHG. *stein* and *gast* from the beginning for both nominative and accusative. The *u* has been better maintained, and we find it after a short syllable in the nominative-accusative *sunu* in Old English, Old Saxon, and Old High German; but after a long syllable, -*u* also disappears: OE. *hond*, OS. *hand*, and OHG. *hant*, opposite Got. *handus* (nom.) and *handu* (acc.), 'hand.'

We must not formulate too rigorous rules for the loss of short vowels in the final syllables of Germanic dialects. For example, we have seen that **-iz* becomes -*s* in Gothic in *gasts*; but where **-iz* (replacing by analogy an ancient **-az*) serves as a nominative-accusative for stems in **-es-*, Gothic has -*is*, and West Germanic keeps the *i*: opposite Skr. *sáhaḥ* (genitive *sáhas-aḥ*), 'power, victory,' we find Got. *sigis*, 'victory,' OE. *sige*, and OS. and OHG. *sigi*. In words of the same class there may be wavering. Thus among the adverbs which have developed from nominative-accusative neuters of the comparative, Gothic has *framis*, 'farther,' but *mins*, 'less' (from **minns*; cf. the comparative *minniza*, 'less,' adjective), *wairs*, 'worse' (cf. *wairsiza*, 'worse,' adjective), and so forth. Wherever **-iz* is reduced to -*s* in a Gothic adverb, the preceding syllable is long; we have seen in Chapter IV that after a long syllable the short syllables disappear more quickly than after a short syllable. However, we do not dare to set up a formula, for Gothic preserves *fotu*, 'foot,' while ancient **burgu*, 'citadel,' becomes Got. *baurg*.

The treatment of long vowels is still more uncertain. To some extent these vowels preserve their long quantity in common Germanic and appear as long in Gothic and Old High German. Others have been shortened since an early date and appear, some in divergent qualities, as short vowels in all dialects. We shall not examine here the unproven hypotheses advanced in recent years to explain these divergences. We shall simply cite a few examples of preserved long vowels beside examples of long vowels which have been shortened. Long vowels in absolute final position all seem to be shortened; on the other hand, long vowels followed by consonants often remain long.

The long final vowels *-ā and *-ō of Indo-European, which were merged in Germanic, are represented at the end of a word by Got. -a and by Nordic and West Germanic -u. The following is a clear example.

For the first-person singular present tense of verbs of the type Gr. *phérō*, 'I carry,' and Lat. *ferō*, Gothic has *baira*, and Old High German has *biru*; the *u* final had disappeared in Old Icelandic, but the old runic Norse still shows *gibu*, 'I give,' like OHG. *gibu*.

On the other hand, ancient *-ā and *-ō are maintained in other cases, notably in the following example where the presence of final *-s will also be observed.

The nominative-accusative plural of stems in -ā-, represented by Skr. -āḥ, Lit. -os (acc. -ās, from *-ós), and Osco-Umbrian -ās (in the nominative only), is shown in Got. *gibos*, OHG. *gebā*, OS. *geba*, and OE. *giefa*. In Scandinavian, we find here in old runic Norse at first -oR—*runoR*, 'runes' —and later -aR—*runaR*; -ar is the form in Old Icelandic.

Before a final nasal, we find the same treatment, except in Old Saxon and in Old High German where -o appears, we do not know why. The genitive plural ending is -ām in Sanskrit and -ôn in Greek; in Gothic we have *gibo*, 'of gifts,' and we have OE. *giefa*, OS. *gebo*, and, likewise, OI. *saka*, 'of things.'

In absolute final position, the *i* of feminines such as Skr. *bṛhati*, 'high,' is shortened; Gothic has forms like *frijondi*, 'friend' (fem.), with short final -i. There is no trace anywhere of -i in this type in Germanic.

In the subjunctives which correspond exactly to the old Latin type *sis* and *sit* (later *sĭt*), we have -i in the second-person singular and -ĭ in the third: Got. *bundeis*, 'that you may have tied,' but *bundi*, 'that he may have tied.' OHG. *buntis* and *bunti* explain the contrast: instead of the ending *-s expected in this form, certain Germanic dialects have borrowed the representative of the ancient *-si of the present, while the third person kept the representative of *-it. Indeed, we know that final *-s is not maintained in West Germanic; Old Saxon has *bundis*, but Old English has the expected *bunde*.

All these actions are complicated and delicate. For the ulterior fate of Germanic they are simple curiosities, because, with time, all the long finals have been shortened: we find only short finals in Old Icelandic and in Old English. Then, in all West Germanic, longs and shorts were reduced to a uniform and neutral type, generally written *e*. This neutral vowel tends to be no longer pronounced. In English, it has disappeared from pronunciation and even from writing: where common Germanic had *bindana(n)*, then *bindan* (in Old German and Old English), English has simply *bind*, while German has *binden*. The vowels of the final syllables of common Germanic were not the only elements to be altered as we have seen; when the shortening of these vowels brought about loss of the vowel, the unaccented vowel of the preceding syllable, finding itself in final position, was submitted to the same mutilations, and, in English, to the same destruction. This simple fact is sufficient to indicate to what point finals have been progressively reduced in West Germanic, and especially in English. This innovation would suffice to give to the language a character quite different from that of ancient Indo-European.

In Celtic, the Gaelic group and the Brythonic group agree in showing a marked reduction of finals, in every way comparable to what we observe in Germanic.

Conclusion to Part One

To GIVE a complete idea of the development of Germanic phonetics, it would be necessary to point out still more details of common Germanic and a few more particularities either of West Germanic or of Nordic. We shall leave aside these facts so as not to blur the lines of the whole.

These special innovations, some of which have been noted incidentally in the course of the exposition, have moreover contributed toward increasing to an even greater extent the difference which has developed between the Indo-European type and the Germanic type.

All the elements of the Indo-European phonic system have been either transformed or seriously modified in Germanic. Often they have changed value because they have taken a place in a new system. An *r* or an *l* in Germanic continues the same phonemes of Indo-European; but these liquids have taken on a different character because they have ceased to alternate with the vocalic forms *r and *l.

Not one of the elements of the Indo-European system has remained in Germanic exactly as it was. The exact conservation of forms, where one seems to see it at first glance, is deceptive. Germanic pronunciation differs radically from Indo-European pronunciation.

On the other hand, the initial principle of each of these great innovations in Germanic has had an exact counterpart in the Celtic languages. Everything has happened as though Germanic and Celtic had undergone the action of languages having the same phonic type, as if Celtic and Germanic had replaced languages articulated in a similar manner. It is not a question of occurrences found in all Western Indo-European languages, for the so-called Italic languages, Latin and Osco-Umbrian, do not participate in these innovations.

PART TWO

MORPHOLOGY

The Effects of Changes in Pronunciation

THE PHONETIC novelties that Germanic introduced were of a nature to overturn the grammatical system and to change the character of the language.

Two of these novelties had a decisive influence: these were the initial accent of intensity and the alteration of finals.

To understand this, it is sufficient to consider the nature of the grammatical structure of Indo-European.

For one thing, syllables were all of equal value in Indo-European, distinguished by a difference in length and by a difference in the pitch of the voice. No syllable put neighboring syllables in the shade. Thus all elements of the word were clear.

The means of expression in Indo-European grammar were three in number: suffixed elements, called suffixes and endings; alternations bearing on the vocalic part of each of the three elements of the word—root, suffix, and ending; and variations in the place of the pitch accent. For example, in the present of the verb "to go," which bears no suffix and has only a root and personal endings, the inflection is first-person singular *éi-mi and first-person plural *i-més, as we see in Skr. émi and imdh, and in Doric Gr. eimi and ímes (this form does not have the accent in the ancient position).

The initial accent of intensity and the extensive alteration of final syllables tended to ruin this system.

In the next chapter we shall return to the consideration of what Germanic kept in the way of vocalic alternations, which is one of the principal means of expression in Indo-European morphology. As a result of the initial accent of intensity, these alternations, which take place in all parts of the word in Indo-European, played a notable role in Germanic only in the first syllable of the word, which was the root syllable. The play of alternations in the inflection has thus been destroyed.

The elimination of the pitch accent, which the initial accent of intensity ruined, suppressed another process in Indo-European grammar. However, we get an idea of this process from the variations in the place of the accent in Lithuanian and in certain Slavic languages, notably Russian and Serbian.

The endings remained, but the alteration of the finals deformed them, changing their appearance and often their character when it did not cause them to disappear entirely. This is the case, for example, with the *-n* of the accusative singular, which has disappeared in all the poly-syllabic words of the Germanic dialects; as a result, in all the words, except the demonstratives (and the adjectives which received the in-flection of the demonstratives), the characteristic of the accusative has been suppressed.

On the other hand, the initial intensity gave prominence to the root, which occupied the first place in the Indo-European word. Thus it came about that the element which expressed the general idea of the word was pronounced with a great intensity, while the rest of the word had an ever decreasing importance. This is the decisive event in the history of Germanic.

Let us examine, for example, a word like the verb meaning "to fill." There was in Indo-European a root *peləð-*, *plē-*, 'to fill'; from this root was formed with the suffix *-no-* an adjective (already pointed out on p. 35), which in the form that serves as immediate antecedent in Germanic was *pḷ-nó-*, 'full' (cf. Lit. *pìlnas*, OSl. *plŭnŭ*, and Skr. *pūrṇáḥ*; cf. also OIr. *lán*; Lat. *plēnus* has another root vowel from the verb *-plēre* of *implēre*, *complēre*); this adjective becomes in Germanic **fulnaz*, from which, after an assimila-tion of *-ln-* to *-ll-*, we get **fullaz*: Got. *fulls* and OHG. *fol(l)*. A derived verb was formed, corresponding to the Slavic *plŭniti*, 'to fill,' as in Got. *fulljan*. Owing as much to the alteration of finals in the adjectives Got. *fulls* and OHG. *fol*, as to the importance acquired by the first accented syllable, Germanic created a radical element *full-*, *foll-*, which is evident in the adjectives Got. *fulls* and OHG. *fol* and in the verbs Got. *fulljan* and OHG. *fullen* (modern Ger. *füllen*).

With the continuation of the degradation of finals, there has remained in a language like English absolutely nothing but the root element: *full*, *fill*. Here, as in many other cases, the radical element of Germanic contains elements foreign to the radical element of Indo-European. The root con-stituted in Germanic becomes the essential element and finally the whole of the word. It is a negation of the Indo-European type.

In some other languages, notably Latin and Irish, the initial accent fell on the preverb where there was one, and the root element under-went alterations from the moment it was no longer the accented element;

to *cadit*, 'he falls,' Latin opposes *ac-cidit*, 'it happens,' or, in the perfect with redoubling, *cecidit*, 'he has fallen.' In Irish, the unaccented syllables have been lost almost since the beginning of tradition, with the result that the radical part of the verb is often unrecognizable. There is nothing of the sort in Germanic. The preverb is never accented before the verb, and consequently the first syllable of the verb, which is the root syllable in derived verbs as in root verbs, is the accented syllable; it still keeps its full clarity, while the preverb became obscured and finally in English even disappeared. Corresponding to the form *ga-tauhans*, 'drawn,' in Gothic, Old High German has *gi-zogan* and modern German has *ge-zogen*. The preverb which in the most ancient Old High German is *ant-* changes to *int-*, then *ent-*; thus we have *ant-fāhan*, then *int-fāhan*, and later *ent-fāhan*, 'to receive,' which in modern German is *empfängen*. The same preverb accented in a derived noun keeps its ancient vowel; Old High German has *ánt-fang*, 'reception,' which has become *empfang* in modern German only because of the influence of the verb *empfangen*. Gothic accented *and-níman*, 'to accept,' but *ánda-nems*, 'accepted,' is the corresponding adjective. The final short vowel of *anda-* disappears in the preverb treated as an autonomous word before the verb which it determines, but it persists in the compound nominal treated as a unit. Modern German has the same adjective, with *ga-* in addition, in the form *an-ge-nehm*; the accent is on the initial syllable with a secondary accent on *-nehm*. Thus it is that the verb forms, which are always accented strongly on the initial syllable and hence clearly show the roots, occupy a dominant place in the language.

The grammatical development of Germanic has then been dominated by two important facts: the initial accent of intensity has given to the roots a new importance; the degradation of the finals has tended to ruin the inflection and has in fact ruined it in languages like English and Danish.

In English, the development has been pushed so far that Germanic words have been reduced largely to the root element, and this radical element, denuded of inflection, often serves at the same time as noun and verb: a word like English *love* is a noun when it is preceded by the article *the*, an infinitive if preceded by *to*, and a verb in the first person of the present if preceded by *I*. The distinction between nominal inflection and verbal inflection, on which the Indo-European grammatical system rests, has thus been abolished.

Chapter VII

Vocalic Alternations

THE VOCALIC alternations, which were one of the fundamental processes of Indo-European morphology, concerned only the two essential vowels of Indo-European, *e* and *o*; they were of the type:

ĕ ē̆ ŏ ō̆   zero.

The same radical element could then appear in the forms *pet-, pēt-, pot , pōt-,* and *pt-*; the same suffix could appear in the forms *-ter-, -tēr-, -tor-, -tōr-,* and *-tr- (-ļ-, -tˣr-),* for example. A Greek verb appears thus in three forms: *leíp-ō,* 'I leave' (in the present), *lé-loip-a,* 'I have left' (in the perfect), and *é-lip-on,* 'I have left' (in the aorist). In Greek we also have in the nominative singular *patḗr,* 'father,' in the accusative *patéra,* in the genitive *patrós,* in the dative plural *patrási* (from **patŗsi*), and so forth. Hence it can be seen that in Indo-European the vowels never characterized roots or suffixes; in all the morphological elements there was basically only one vowel, which appeared as *ĕ, ē, ŏ, ō,* or zero, according to the type of word formation and grammatical form. The consonants and sonants were the only true constituents of roots and suffixes; the vowels were simply grammatical tools, similar to the suffixes or endings.

The rigor of this principle is tempered by certain facts which depart from it or which deviate from it at least in appearance. The vowel **ă* does not figure in any alternation: therefore, a root like that of Skr. *ájāmi,* 'I conduct,' Gr. *ágō,* Lat. *agō,* Arm. *acem,* or OI. *aka,* 'to conduct,' escapes all alternation; the *ē* of the Lat. perfect *ēgi,* and the *ō* of the OI. preterite *ōk* are particularities of a single language, and there is no correspondence between Latin *ē* and Scandinavian *ō*. Alternations of the types *ē, ō, ə,* or *ā, ə,* or *ō, ə* basically belong to the general type, but, to judge from the evidence for alternations in Indo-European, they are exceptional; they are however parallel to the alternations of the general type.

In Germanic, vocalic alternations have persisted clearly only in root syllables. In other parts of the word, there are still traces of vocalic alternations, examples of which we shall see in the course of the study of inflection. However, they are no longer true alternations, discernible in Germanic.

Even in the root syllable, the alternations have lost the unity they had in Indo-European; and the alterations of the true vowels and of the sonants have given them a new aspect.

Between two true consonants or initially before a true consonant, the ancient alternation has been maintained in the Germanic form:

$$e/i \quad \bar{e} \quad a \, \bar{o} \quad \text{(zero)}.$$

The zero degree is shown only in isolated cases because it involves accumulations of consonants. The alternation *e/i, ē, a* is usual in strong verbs. It is the type:

Got.	*giban*	*gaf*	*gebun*
	'to give'	'he gave'	'they gave'
OHG.	*gibu*		
	'I give'		
	gebant	*gab*	*gābun*
	'they give'		

It will be noticed that an alternation of Germanic creation, *e/i*, has been added in Nordic and West Germanic to the alternations inherited from Indo-European.

The alternation *ō/a* exists where the present has the root vowel *a* (ancient *o* or ancient *a*), as, for example, in Got. *graban*, 'to dig,' preterite *grof*, 'he dug,' and in OHG. *graban, gruob*. It is only by exception that the Germanic alternation *ō/a* is based upon an Indo-European alternation *ā/∂* (or *ō/∂*); we have a sure example in the Got. preterite *stoþ*, 'he stood,' from *standan*, opposite Lat. *stāre*, 'to stand,' and *status*, and Skr. *á-sthā-t*, 'he stood,' and *sthi-táh*, 'standing.'

As soon as a sonant intervenes, there are complications.

The alternation

ei	*oi*	*i*,

to which the whole system is limited when a true consonant follows *i*, becomes in Germanic:

i	*ai*	*e/i*.

Thus we have:

Got.	*beitan*	*bait*	*bitun*
	'to bite'	'he bit'	'they bit'
OHG.	*bizzan*	*beiz*	*bizzun*

In the passive past participle we have by analogy OHG. *gi-bizzan*, with *i* instead of the expected *e*. Opposite OHG. *stīgan*, 'to mount,' *steig*, and *stigun*, the *e* appears in the substantive OHG. *steg*, 'path,' corresponding to OI. *stigr*.

In like manner, before a true consonant we have:

eu   *ou*   *u.*

This alternation is represented in Germanic by

iu/io   *au*   *u/o,*

with Gothic having naturally only *iu*, *au* (diphthong), and *u* (*au* notation for short *o* before *h* and *r*):

Got.	*biudan*	*bauþ*	*budun*
	'I order'	'he ordered'	'they ordered'
OHG.	*biotan*	*bōt*	*butun*

(1st-pers. pres., *biutu*) (passive past part., *gi-botan*)

In Old High German *au* becomes *ō* before a dental.

When the sonants *r*, *l*, *n*, and *m* precede a true consonant, we find parallel treatment of the Indo-European type:

er   *or*   *ŗ*

In Germanic this becomes:

er/ir   *ar*   *ur/or*
el/il   *al*   *ul/ol*
in   *an*   *un*
im   *am*   *um*

Hence we have:

Got.	*wairþan*	*warþ*	*waurþun*
	'to become'	'he became'	'they became'
OHG.	*werdan*	*ward*	*wurtun*

(1st-pers. sg., *wirdu*) (passive past part., *wortan*)

OI.	*verda*	*varð*	

Got.	*hilpan*	*halp*	*hulpun*
	'to help'	'he helped'	'they helped'
OHG.	*helfan*	*half*	*hulfun*

(1st-pers. sg., *hilfu*) (passive past part., *gi-holfan*)

Got.	*bindan*	*band*	*bundun*
	'to tie'	'he tied'	'they tied'

OI.	*binda*	*batt*	*bundu*
OHG.	*bintan*	*bant*	*buntun*

(passive past part., *gi-buntan*)

When one of the sonants *r*, *l*, *n*, or *m* precedes a vowel, the facts are more complicated. The alternation appears in Indo-European with the forms:

er	*ēr*	*or*	*ōr*	*r̥* (*ṛ*)

In Germanic this becomes:

er/ir	*ēr*	*ar*	*ōr*	*ur/or*
el/il	*ēl*	*al*	*ōl*	*ul/ol*
en/in	*ēn*	*an*	*ōn*	*un/on*
em/im	*ēm*	*am*	*ōm*	*um/om*

In the verbs which have the root vowel ancient *e* in the present, we find represented the alternations *er/ir*, *ēr/ar*, and *ur/or*:

Got.	*bairan*	*bar*	*berun*	*baurans*
	'to carry'	'he carried'	'they carried'	'carried'
OI.	*bera*	*bar*	*bǫro*	*borenn*
OHG.	*beran*	*bar*	*bārun*	*gi-boran*

(1st-pers. sg., *biru*)

Got.	*stilan*	*stal*	*stelun*	*stulans*
	'to steal'	'he stole'	'they stole'	'stolen'
OHG.	*stelan*	*stal*	*stālun*	*gi-stolan*

Got.	*niman*	*nam*	*nemun*	*numans*
	'to take'	'he took'	'they took'	'taken'
OI.	*nema*	*nam*	*nǫmo*	*numenn* (and *nomenn*)
OHG.	*neman*	*nam*	*nāmun*	*gi-noman*

(1st-pers. sg., *nimu*)

Verbs which have in the present the root vowel *-a-*, representing an ancient *-o-*, offer only a quantitative alternation *ŏ/ō*, that is, in Germanic *a/ō*: for example, Got. *faran*, 'to drive a vehicle,' preterite *for*, 'I, he drove'; OI. *fara*, *fōr*; and OHG. *faran*, *fuor*.

There are only isolated traces of the Indo-European alternation *ā*, *ō*, *ǝ*, of which one of the most curious examples is Got. *letan*, 'to let, to lend' (preterite with redoubling, *lailot*), beside the adjectives Got. *lats*, 'cowardly,' OI. *latr*, and OHG. *laz*, in which *a* comes from IE. *ǝ*.

The preceding examples have been borrowed systematically from strong verbs. However, insofar as the same root elements figure in nominal formations, they necessarily appear in them with a vowel which represents one of the alternation types. We have already seen one or two examples incidentally. Here are a few others. Beside Got. *ga-timan*, 'to be suitable,' OS. *teman*, and OHG. *zeman* (1st-pers. sg., *zimu*), and Got. *ga-tamjan*, 'to tame,' OI. *temia*, and OHG. *zemmen* (cf. Lat. *domāre*, 'to subdue'), we have the adjectives OI. *tamr* and OHG. *zam*, 'tame.' Beside Got. *bairan*, 'to carry,' and OHG. *beran* (modern Ger. *ge-bären*, 'to give birth'), we have Got. *ga-baurþs*, OI. *burðr*, and OHG. *gi-burt*, 'birth'; here we notice the type *ṛ* before a consonant, which does not figure in the forms of the corresponding strong verb. Beside Got. *kann*, 'he understands,' OI. *kann*, and OHG. *kan*, we find OHG. *kuoni*, 'bold,' OE. *cēne* (*ē* representing *ō* before ancient *i* of the following syllable), and OI. *kønn*, 'wise, experienced.' The nominal forms of this sort are numerous, but they do not constitute a system such as we find in the strong verb. The feeling for the alternations tends then to be effaced, as does even the feeling of relationship among the words of the group. Almost all that remains in Germanic of the feeling for the ancient alternations of the vowels relates to the strong verb type.

The partial maintenance of vocalic alternations is an archaism in Germanic. However, as a result of the changes in the vowels and the sonants, Germanic offers several more or less parallel and distinct types of alternations, whereas Indo-European had only one type. Moreover, the alternations *e/i* and *u/o*, which appear in West Germanic and Nordic and which are a Germanic creation, bring to the system a new complication.

Chapter VIII

Change of Grammatical Type

No INDO-EUROPEAN language known at a date comparable to that of Germanic has faithfully preserved the grammatical type of common Indo-European. Even Vedic Sanskrit, the Iranian of the Gathas of the Avesta, and Homeric Greek give us only a weakened idea of it. Germanic, disturbed by the intensity of initial syllables and the weakening of finals, inevitably transformed a grammatical system so delicate and so extraordinarily complicated as was that of Indo-European.

However, common Germanic, which had not as yet been subjected to much alteration of finals, shows an inflection which is relatively archaic. This archaism, still discernible in old runic Norse and in Gothic, diminished rapidly with time. No West Germanic dialect is known in an archaic form that is still close to the common Germanic type.

The essential trait of the Indo-European system is the necessity of showing a grammatical feature in every form of a word. In English there is the word "house." In Indo-European there was a form of this word in the nominative singular, Greek *dōmos*, 'house,' and Skr. *dámaḥ*; a form in the accusative singular, Gr. *dómon* and Skr. *dámam*; a form in the accusative plural, Gr. *dómous* and Skr. *dámān*; and so forth. Nothing without a grammatical characteristic signified "house." For the word "father," there was a nominative singular, Gr. *patḗr*, Lat. *pater*, and Skr. *pitá*; a dative singular, Gr. *patrí*, Lat. *patri*, and Skr. *pitré*; and so on. There was nowhere a form that signified simply "father." We call "stem" that element which carries the meaning of the word and to which are added the endings which mark the number and case for the noun, the person for the verb, and so forth. However, the stems do not exist in isolation; they appear only with special forms of inflection. Stems like *dómo-* or *patér-* are not words like "house" or "father"; moreover, the vowels vary with the forms. Thus, the stem is not just *domo-*, but *domo-* or *dome-*; not just *patér-*, but *patér-*, *patér-*, *patr-* (*patr-*), and so on.

Thus it is that we can recognize always at first glance, by inspecting the form, whether a given Indo-European word is a noun or a verb. The forms of the noun are, in fact, entirely distinct from those of the verb. On the other hand, the Germanic language which presents the most advanced development, English, hardly distinguishes noun from verb any longer, and, as has already been noted, a word like *love* is either a noun or a verb depending on the little words that go with it and the way in which it is used in the sentence.

As far back as the time of the earliest extant monuments of Germanic, the inflection is simplified.

Entire categories have disappeared as in other Indo-European languages.

Thus the dual number is replaced by the plural in the nominal inflection, and the dual remains distinct from the plural only in verb forms and personal pronouns in old runic Norse and Gothic. These vestiges of the use of the dual are eliminated in their turn, and neither Old Icelandic nor the West Germanic dialects have any forms of the dual in the verb. The only traces of the dual in ancient West Germanic are found in the personal pronoun. Ultimately the dual category was completely eliminated.

In the verb, there were two moods in Indo-European opposed to the indicative, the subjunctive and the optative; Germanic has kept only one which we call the subjunctive and which is based on the Indo-European optative.

Likewise, the distinction between the perfect and the aorist has been eliminated in the verb. In the noun, the number of case forms has been reduced.

In all this there is nothing peculiar to Germanic; similar developments have taken place throughout the Indo-European domain. We can even say that Germanic was for a long time conservative in morphology. For example, it retained important vestiges of the dual at a time when Greek, Latin, the languages of India, and Persian no longer had any; and this is not surprising, since the disappearance of the dual is a development of civilization. The case inflection of Germanic in the fourth century A.D. is not less rich than that of Homeric Greek; in some respects it is even richer; thus the inflection of the demonstrative has remained distinct from that of the substantive. It is the phonetic ruin of the finals which precipitated the simplification of the inflection.

What gave Indo-European inflection a particularly involved aspect was the fact that the characteristics of the grammatical categories varied according to number and according to the stems. A genitive, for example, is not indicated by the same ending in the singular, the plural, and the dual. Moreover, the genitive is not expressed in the same way in the singular with a stem in -*o*-, such as that of Skr. *vŕkasya*, 'of the wolf,' and Homeric *lýkoio*, as it is with a stem in -*u*-, such as that of Skr. *sūnóḥ*, 'of the son,' and Lit. *sūnaũs*, or with a stem terminating in a consonant, such as that of Skr. *padáḥ*, 'of the foot,' and Gr. *podós*. This variety of forms for a single and same grammatical category is one of the original traits of Indo-European.

Like all Indo-European languages, Germanic kept distinct characteristics for the same categories in the singular and in the plural. However, like the other languages of the group, it tended to restrict the variety of inflections for the various types of words. The rarest types tended to adopt the characteristics of the most usual types. For example, the masculine stems in -*i*- became similar to the forms with stems in -*a*- (Indo-European type in -*o*-).

In this way, Germanic simplified the inflection in the same direction as the other Indo-European languages.

There were two principal types of inflection in Indo-European, one for stems terminating in a vowel *e/o*, the other for stems terminating in a consonant like -*d*- or -*s*- or in a sonant like -*y*- (-*i*-), -*r*- (-*ṛ*-), and so forth. Germanic, like most languages, tended to generalize the type ending in a vowel, called "thematic" type, at the expense of the other type, called "athematic." In the present tense of verbs of the thematic type, the first-person singular was in *-ō*, thus Gr. *phérō*, 'I carry,' while that of the athematic type was in *-mi*, thus Skr. *asmi*, 'I am,' and Gr. *eimi* (from *esmi*). The type in *-mi* tended to be eliminated, and the present *im*, 'I am,' is the only form which persists in the ensemble of Germanic dialects of a type whose importance in Indo-European balanced that of the thematic type.

In the nouns, the athematic inflection was better preserved than in the verbs. The type of stems ending in -*n*- acquired a great importance and furnished what is called the "weak" inflection, one of the normal and productive types in Germanic.

Some details show that even noun stems ending in an occlusive kept their ancient character in common Germanic. Take, for example, the noun for "tooth," which is in Sanskrit nom. sg. *dán*, acc. sg. *dántam*, and gen. sg. *datáḥ*. Germanic had an inflection with vocalic alternations in the syllable preceding the ending, just as in Sanskrit; thus we have acc. sg. *tanþu(n)*, from *dónt-ṇ* (cf. Skr. *dántam* and Gr. (*o*)*dónta*), and gen. sg. *tunþiz*, from *dṇt-és* (cf. Skr. *datáḥ* and Lat. *dentis*). Then the Germanic dialects normalized the root vowel; Gothic generalized *un*, and the accusative *tunþu*, thus obtained, brought about the change of inflection to the type for stems in -*u*-, gen. *tunþaus*, and so forth, while West Germanic and Nordic generalized *an*, as in acc. sg. OI. *tǫnn*, OE. *tōd*, and OHG.

zan(t), and gen. sg. OI. *tannar*, OE. *tōdes*, and OHG. *zandes*. The ancient nominative plural *dónt-es (Skr. *dántah* and Gr. *(o)dóntes*) is preserved in OI. *tedr* (and *tennr*) and OE. *tēd* (English *teeth* beside the singular *tooth*). The effects of the variations in the position of the pitch accent attested by Skr. *dántam* and *datáh* are no longer perceptible in Germanic; the *þ preserved phonetically in the forms where the accent was on the initial syllable was generalized; nowhere is there a trace of the *d which, according to Verner's Law, would be expected in the genitive *tunþiz, which ought to be phonetically *tundiz. The opposition between the Gothic forms and those of other dialects shows that the athematic type with its alternations was conserved in common Germanic in this word and doubtless in others. There are various other traces in the Germanic languages.

On the whole, however, the thematic type prevailed.

In the athematic type, the root part of the word, which we call the stem, and the endings are clearly distinct; thus we have acc. sg. Skr. *dánt-am*, Gr. *(o)dónta*, Lat. *dent-em*, and common Germanic **tanþ-u(n)*, and gen. sg. Skr. *dat-áh*, Gr. *(o)dónt-os*, Lat. *dent-is*, and common Germanic *tunþ-iz (replacing *tund-iz).

In the thematic type, on the contrary, the stem and the endings are often fused, and the two elements are no longer discernible; there is no way of separating the stem and the ending in a dative singular of the thematic type such as Avestan *vǝkrkāi*, 'to the wolf,' Lit. *vilkui*, Gr. *lýkōi*, and Lat. *lupō*, for example. In instances where the stem and the ending can be isolated on paper, as in the acc. sg. Skr. *vŕka-m*, 'wolf,' Gr. *lýko-n*, and Lat. *lupu-m*, the two elements are so united in pronunciation that they form a single final. A thematic inflection of common Germanic such as that of nom. sg. *armaz, 'arm,' acc. sg. **arma(n)*, gen. sg. **armes(a)* (soon reduced to *armes), and so on, tends then to be cut *arm-az, **arm-a(n)*, and *arm-es, and Germanic tends to separate the root *arm-*, which expresses the idea of "arm," from the finals *-*az*, *-*a(n)*, and *-*es*, which mark the inflection of the word.

From the thematic type, this conception of the forms has extended to the athematic type. Thus the finals of the stems in *-*u*-, which were from the Indo-European point of view athematic, and which were cut *-*u-s*, *-*u-n*, and *-*ou-s*, were conceived as finals of the thematic type and were cut as follows: nom. sg. *sun-uz, 'son,' acc. sg. **sun-u(n)*, gen. sg. *sun-auz, and so forth. Thereafter, on an accusative singular such as common Germanic **fōt-u(n)*, 'foot,' which is of the same type as Skr. *pád-am*, Gr. *pód-a*, and Lat. *ped-em*, a whole inflection was formed: nom. sg. *fōt-uz and gen. sg. *fōt-auz. This inflection is that of Got. *fotus*, *fotu*, and *fotaus*, for example. These analogic creations show what a change occurred in the conception of forms. The final of the Got. acc. *fotu* corresponds phonetically to that of Gr. *póda* or that of Lat. *pedem*; but, from the grammatical point of view, it was conceived differently by the speaker.

The finals were shortened and altered. Thus, in Gothic, we find the inflection *armaz, *arma(n), *armes represented by *arms*, *arm*, *armis*. West Germanic, in which the *-*z* final disappears, is still more characteristic: it has nom.-acc. sg. *arm* and gen. sg. *armes*. All feeling for the vowel which terminated the stem disappears. On the one hand, the word *arm*, 'arm,' is constituted; this word exists in isolation, and, without any ending, it serves as the nominative-accusative singular and bears the accent. On the other hand, characteristic case finals, which are pronounced less and less clearly, tend to disappear.

Thus a complete change in the manner of conceiving forms began to take place in common Germanic and materialized in the course of history in each of the various Germanic dialects. Even where they represent ancient Indo-European forms exactly, the Germanic forms, from the time of the most ancient texts, are in reality something quite different. The Indo-European word was also at the same time a grammatical form, constituted by the union of a stem and an ending. It materialized, so to speak, the notion to be expressed, furnishing it with indications of number, gender, and case or of person, voice, and so on, which made it a whole sufficient unto itself. In Germanic, on the contrary, the tendency was to create a word independent of any grammatical form. The final became an accessory, still playing an important role in common Germanic, but progressively losing its significance and little by little disappearing. If some text should reveal common Germanic to the linguist, it would undoubtedly be thought to show a grammatical type still similar to the Indo-European type in general. This would be an illusion: common Germanic already presented features which were to lead to a new morphologic type. While less apparent at first glance, this revolution has been as significant as the one we have observed in phonetics.

A similar tendency is noticeable from an early date in Celtic. From the time of the most ancient texts, case inflection was abolished in Brythonic.

Chapter IX

The Verb

A. Generalities

THE INDO-EUROPEAN verb had a structure quite different from that found in most of the attested languages of the Germanic group, even in those for which we have the most ancient texts.

If we examine a Latin verb, we see that it is composed of two groups of personal forms, the "infectum" group—*dicō*, 'I say,' *amō*, 'I love'—and the "perfectum" group—*dixi*, 'I have said,' *amāui*, 'I have loved'; we must add a nominal form, the participle—*dictus*, 'said,' *amātus*, 'loved.' The ensemble of these three groups and of all the forms related to them constitutes what is called the "conjugation" of a Latin verb. The same two groups of personal forms occur in all verbs, with the same oppositions of meanings and with analogous formations. On the one hand, we have the group *dicō*, 'I say,' *dicam*, 'I shall say' (*dicēs*, 'you will say'), and *dicēbam*, 'I was saying,' or *amō*, 'I love,' *amābō*, 'I shall love,' and *amābam*, 'I was loving'; on the other hand, we have the group *dixi*, 'I have said,' *dixerō*, 'I shall have said,' and *dixeram*, 'I had said,' or *amāui*, 'I have loved,' *amāuerō*, 'I shall have loved,' and *amāueram*, 'I had loved.' The conjugation of a Latin verb is thus something rigidly determined in meaning and in form.

If, on the contrary, we examine an Indo-Iranian verbal group, we see that from each root multiple formations appear, all of which are independent of one another, and none of which permits us to foresee what other forms will be. In Vedic the present formations are extremely varied: *ásti*, 'he is,' *dádāti*, 'he gives,' *bhinátti*, 'he splits,' *vindáti*, 'he finds,' *pṛṇáti*, 'he fills,' *stṛṇóti*, 'he spreads,' *bhárati*, 'he carries,' *tudáti*, 'he jostles,' *páçyati*, 'he sees,' *pṛccháti*, 'he questions,' and *mṛṇáti*, 'he crushes,' furnish examples each of a distinct type, and we have not taken any notice of intensives like *nénekti*, 'he washes,' or of desideratives like *nínitsati*, 'he wishes to outrage.' Moreover, the same root may furnish several presents; thus Sanskrit has both *bhárati* and *bíbharti*, 'he carries,' Greek has both *ménō* and *mímnō*, 'I remain,' Latin has both *stō*, 'I stand,' and *sistō*, 'I stop,' and so forth. No form of the present permits predicting either the existence of an aorist or a perfect or the form of this aorist. Consequently, verbs formed from nouns by means of a derivational suffix never supply more than a single stem, which is a present stem. For example, a Sanskrit present derived from a word meaning "master" (cf. Skr. *pátiḥ*, 'master'), *pátyate*, 'he is master of' (cf. Lat. *potitur*, 'he takes possession of'), has no aorist, no perfect, no future; we only have the present, *pátyate*.

A comparison with other languages and in particular with Homeric Greek shows that the ancient Indo-Iranian verb faithfully represents the Indo-European type in its general features. There is a conjugation in ancient Greek and, with simpler forms, in Latin, Irish, Lithuanian, Slavic, Armenian, and so on. However, the structural peculiarities of the conjugation vary from one language to another; the conjugation has been fixed independently in each Indo-European language. We cannot therefore explain the conjugation of a language by comparing it with that of another language of the group; we must always refer back to the Indo-European type of verb, which has strictly autonomous stems attached directly to the verbal root, or which has a single stem if it is a question of a derived verb.

The Germanic conjugation is one of the most clearly defined. It is simple, and its forms present a rigorous parallelism. As in the Latin conjugation, each verb has two stems and a past participle with intransitive or passive value; root verbs and derived verbs both have their two stems and their participles. Thus, in Gothic we have the root verb *binda*, 'I bind,' *band*, 'I have bound, he has bound,' *bundun*, 'they have bound,' and *bundans*, 'bound,' and we have the derived verb *salbo*, 'I anoint,' *salboda*, 'I have anointed, he has anointed,' and *salboþs*, 'anointed.' One who knows these three forms of a Germanic verb knows how to conjugate the entire verb, exactly as we are able to conjugate the entire Latin verb *dire* when we know *dīcō (dicis)*, *dixi*, *dictus*. This structure of the verb has its equivalent in several other languages of the Indo-European group, but it represents something new compared with the common Indo-European type.

The novelty of the Germanic type does not bear just on the form; there is also novelty in meaning.

The stems of Indo-European verbs expressed not time but the aspect under which the action was considered. A Greek present like *leípo* means 'I am in the act of leaving,' and a Greek perfect like *léloipa* means 'I have accomplished the action of leaving, and I have the results at hand'; an imperfect like *éleipon* (which belongs to the group of the "present") means 'I was, or I have been in the act of leaving,' while an aorist like *élipon* indicates purely and simply the historic fact that 'I left'; the future *leípso* meant originally 'I wish to leave': it is an ancient desiderative. The notion of the past was expressed in Indo-European not by the form of the stem but by the form of the endings: thus, in the Greek of Homer, *leípō* means 'I leave,' and *leípon* means 'I left.'

In Germanic, on the contrary, the verbal stems express the opposition of the present and the past: Got. *binda* means 'I bind,' and *band* means 'I bound'; *salbo* means 'I anoint,' and *salboda* means 'I anointed'; and thus it is always. The difference in inflection is only added to the difference in the form of the stem.

In Greek, an optative aorist like *lípoi*, 'he can leave,' has no more preterite value than an optative present like *leípoi*, 'he can leave'; the first expresses the process pure and simple, the second the process which continues; but between the two there is no difference in time indicated. In Germanic, however, a subjunctive (ancient optative) Got. *bundi*, 'that he may have bound,' has a preterite value in contrast with the subjunctive (ancient optative) Got. *bindai*, 'that he may bind.'

Putting time in the first rank of notions expressed by verbal stems is a novelty which characterizes Germanic, Celtic, and Italic.

Unlike Latin, where within each principal stem of the verb there is an opposition of three tenses, present, past, and future, as in the "infectum" group *dicō*, 'I say,' *dicēbam*, 'I was saying,' and *dicam*, 'I shall say,' and in the "perfectum' group *dixi*, 'I have said,' *dixeram*, 'I had said,' and *dixerō*, 'I shall have said,' Germanic does not give expression to the future. In the course of their development, Germanic languages have never succeeded in producing a distinct future. The expression of time has remained limited to the opposition of the present (the forms of which also serve for the future) and the past.

The Indo-European usage of having a preterite that expresses an action which continued in the past beside an action which is being developed in the present, as in Gr. *éleipon*, 'I was leaving,' beside *leípō*, 'I am leaving,' was eliminated in Germanic. Germanic has nothing similar to the Greek or Sanskrit imperfect or to the Latin imperfect, which moreover is a new form.

In Indo-European, where the verbal stem expressed the aspect of the envisaged action, each stem had an imperative; thus Greek opposes the present imperative *leípe*, 'be in the act of leaving,' to the aorist imperative *lípe*, 'leave' (pure and simple). In Germanic, only the present imperative persists; there is an imperative Got. *bind*, 'bind,' and *salbo*, 'anoint,' opposite the present *binda*, 'I bind,' and *salbo*, 'I anoint.' For the preterites *band*, 'I have bound,' and *salboda*, 'I have anointed,' there are no corresponding imperatives.

In a language like Indo-European, where the word exists only with a special grammatical form, an infinitive which serves to indicate the general idea of the verb independent of any grammatical category scarcely had a place. However, with the change of type, an infinitive was constituted in Germanic, as it was in most languages. Since the present no longer expressed a particular aspect of an action, the infinitive became attached to the present group. Infinitives then were created which belonged in form to the present group but which were basically neither present nor past, expressing rather the general idea of the verb: Got. *bindan*, 'to bind,' *salbon*, 'to anoint.'

Germanic also simplified the verbal system by eliminating the opposition of active endings and middle endings. In accordance with the relation of the action expressed to the subject, active or middle endings were used in Indo-European: the active Gr. *leipō* means 'I leave,' while the middle Gr. *leípomai* means 'I leave for myself' or 'I am left.' Germanic knew this opposition. Gothic still used it in the present where the ancient middle endings express the passive: *bairiþ*, which corresponds to Skr. *bhárati*, 'he carries,' has this same meaning; *bairada*, which should be compared with Skr. *bhárate* and Gr. *phéretai*, 'he carries for himself' and 'he is carried,' means 'he is carried.' The other Germanic dialects have lost the middle inflection of the present. In the preterite, Gothic itself does not have the middle endings.

Indo-European had a complete system of participles; each verb stem had its own participle, that is, a form built on this stem but furnished with a case inflection, which was consequently both verbal and nominal. Inasmuch as Indo-European had a double set of endings, there were two participles for each stem, one active, the other middle. Thus in Greek we have beside *leipō*, 'I leave,' the participle *leípōn*, 'leaving' (acc. sg. *leíponta*), and beside *leípomai*, 'I leave for myself, I am left,' the participle *leipómenos*, 'leaving for oneself, being left'; beside *léloipa*, 'I have left,' the participle *leloipós*, 'having left,' and beside *léleimmai*, 'I have been left,' the participle *leleimménos*, 'having been left'; and so forth. Of this system which is so rich and so complete, Germanic has kept only the present active participle such as the Got. *bindands*, 'binding,' and *salbonds*, 'anointing.' The few perfect active participles that persisted in Gothic became substantives: *weitwops*, 'witness' (literally, 'who knows'), is an ancient perfect participle which corresponds to Gr. *weidós*, 'knowing.' This shows that the perfect participle was perpetuated down to common Germanic.

On the other hand, the adjectives in *-to-* and in *-no-*, which in Indo-European were either roots or derived from nouns, furnished Germanic, Celtic, and Latin with a large category of intransitive or passive participles.

Latin has beside *-plēo, -plēre,* 'to fill,' both *-plētus,* 'filled,' and *plēnus,* 'full.' The type in *-tus* has been incorporated in the verb: Lat. *dictus,* 'said,' is one of the constituent elements of the conjugation of *dicō,* 'I say.' Germanic has likewise incorporated these adjectives in the verbs, and thus we have Got. *bundans,* 'bound,' and *salboþs,* 'anointed.'

In this manner then was the conjugation of common Germanic constituted. Each verb normally consisted of three groups of forms:

1. The present group: present indicative, present subjunctive, imperative, present participle, and infinitive (the imperative and the infinitive not having properly the value of the present).

2. The preterite group: preterite indicative and preterite subjunctive.

3. The intransitive or passive past participle.

The following examples, all Gothic and cited in the third-person singular for the personal forms other than the imperative, illustrate the system.

Verb *niman,* 'to take':

1. Present group: *nimiþ,* 'he takes,' *nimai,* 'that he may take,' *nim,* 'take,' *nimands,* 'taking,' and *niman,* 'to take.'

2. Preterite group: *nam,* 'he has taken' (3rd pl., *nemun*), and *nemi,* 'that he may have taken.'

3. Passive past participle: *numans,* 'taken.'

Verb *sokjan,* 'to seek':

1. Present group: *sokeiþ,* 'he seeks,' *sokjai,* 'that he may seek,' *sokei,* 'seek,' *sokjands,* 'seeking,' and *sokjan,* 'to seek.'

2. Preterite group: *sokida,* 'he has sought,' and *sokidedi,* 'that he may have sought.'

3. Passive past participle: *sokiþs,* 'sought.'

The passive past participle played a considerable role: joined to the verb "to be," it served to render the passive preterite. Thus, in Gothic, where the passive is rendered in the present by the ancient middle forms, the passive preterite is rendered by the participle with auxiliary; for example, Gr. *errḗthē,* 'it has been said,' is translated by *qiþan ist.* This process is found in all of the other Germanic languages; in addition to the use of the verb "to be," combinations were also formed with the verb "to become," OI. *verda,* OHG. *werdan.*

An important procedure, not yet utilized by Gothic and doubtlessly owing in the beginning to imitation of Vulgar Latin models, is that which consists of uniting the participle with the verb "to have." At a time when the terms of a locution such as Lat. *ego habeo aliquem amatum,* 'I have someone that I love' (literally, 'I have someone loved'), were still felt separately, this very expressive phrase might have been copied by the speakers of Germanic who knew Latin and might have been reproduced in the Germanic world. We already find in Old High German examples such as *dū habēst irslagan*, 'you have brought down,' and in Old Icelandic examples such as *ek hefe kallat*, 'I have called.' With time this process acquired more and more importance, and forms of the modern German type such as *ich habe erschlagen* have entirely supplanted the simple preterites like *ich erschlug* in a majority of present-day German dialects, just as *j'ai abattu* has supplanted the type *j'abattis* in current modern French usage. Here we see a new development which draws the language in a direction opposite to that of the common Indo-European type.

B. The Strong Verb

From ancient Indo-Iranian, from Greek, and from all that has come down to us from other sources, we know that the principal Indo-European verbs were composed of forms attached directly to "roots"; the presents derived from nouns formed only a small part of the verb category in ancient Indo-European languages. These diverse root formations are still numerous in the attested languages of ancient date such as Greek or Latin. Languages of a relatively archaic type like Old Irish still preserve a large number of root forms, and there are still many of them in Germanic.

What is original in Germanic is that the root verbs have been constituted in a well-defined type; they are called "strong verbs." Not all strong verbs are formed in exactly the same way. However, except for a small number of unusual cases, they belong to a type which is based on a single Indo-European type, while in most other languages there are remains of more or less diverse formations without organization of the root type.

The present is of the type called "thematic" in Indo-European, which has presents in the first-person active singular in -ō, as in Avestan *barā*, 'I carry,' Gr. *phérō*, Lat. *ferō*, and so on; similarly, in Gothic this verb form is *baira*. This type, with root vowel *e* and an accent on this *e*, is the one which has been best maintained in most languages. However, no other Indo-European language has given it as much extension as Germanic.

On the one hand, Germanic has preserved many of these presents of Indo-European date: Gr. *leípō*, 'I leave' (infinitive, *leípein*), Lit. *lëkù* (cf. Got. *leihwa*, 'I lend'),[1] Lat. *dūcō* (from **deukō*), 'I lead' (cf. Got. *tiuha*), Skr.

---

1. Strong verbs are found for the most part in all ancient Germanic dialects, or at least in several. Unless there are special reasons, they will be cited always in a single language, usually Gothic.

vártate, 'he turns,' Lat. *uerto* (cf. Got. *wairþa*, 'I become'—literally, 'I turn myself around').

On the other hand, and here is the novelty, Germanic has brought into this type of thematic presents verbs which had another structure. For example, a present like Got. *binda*, 'I bind,' has no exact equivalent outside of Germanic; Sanskrit has a present with this root, *badhnáti*, 'he binds,' but this was surely formed in a secondary manner. A present like Got. *brika*, 'I break,' likewise has no equivalent outside Germanic; Latin has a quite different type, *frangō*. The present Got. *beita*, 'I bite,' is parallel to differently constituted and more archaic presents: Skr. *bhinádmi*, 'I split,' and Lat. *findō*. The root **gheu-*, 'to pour,' which undoubtedly furnished an athematic present in Indo-European, received a secondary suffix, **-de-*, thanks to which a present of thematic type, Got. *giuta*, 'I pour,' was constituted with the aspect of a root present; the Lat. *fundō* has a different structure but uses the same suffix.

In certain cases we see clearly how the thematic present developed. We may take, for example, Got. *winna*, 'I suffer' (a comparison of Germanic dialects indicates that the meaning of this present in common Germanic was 'I struggle, I obtain by struggle'). The *-nn-* cannot be ancient, for gemination in Indo-European never occurred in a present of this sort. The *-nn-* is based on an ancient **-nw-*; indeed, the Indo-Iranian stem has the form **wanau-*: Skr. *vanóti*, 'he obtains, he earns,' or, with middle ending, *vanuté*, 'he earns for himself.' The Germanic present is based on **wenwe-*, developed from **wenu-*.

More than one form of the athematic type changed to the thematic type. Thus, from the root **ed-*, 'to eat,' Indo-European had an athematic present: Skr. *ádmi*, Lit. *édmi*, and so forth. Under the influence of the third-person plural and of the present participle, which are similar to forms of the thematic type, as in Lat. *edunt* and Lat. *edens* (cf. Skr. *adánti*, 'they eat,' and *adán*, 'eating'), Latin developed present forms in part thematic, *edō*, 'I eat,' *edimus*, 'we eat,' beside athematic forms, *ēs*, 'you eat,' *ēst*, 'he eats,' and so on. In Germanic the change to the thematic type is complete in Got. *itan*, 'to eat,' OI. *eta*, OE. *etan*, and OHG. *ezzan*, and nothing proclaims the ancient Indo-European type.

The fact that some presents of strong verbs have secondarily entered this type is manifested sometimes by differences in the forms of the Germanic dialects. The athematic presents of the athematic root type oppose in the prefinal syllable the vowel *e* in the singular to zero in the plural, and there are at the same time variations in the placing of the accent; thus we have Skr. *émi*, 'I go,' Gr. *eîmi*, and Skr. *imáḥ*, 'we go,' Doric Gr. *ímes* (with accent displaced). An isolated example of this type has been maintained in Germanic where we have Got. *ist,* 'he is' (cf. Skr. *ásti,* Gr. *ésti,* and Lat. *est*), and Got. *sind,* 'they are' (ancient atonic form) (cf. Skr. *santi,* Doric Gr. *enti,* Oscan *sent,* and Lat. *sunt*). There was undoubtedly also in Indo-European a present **wéik-mi,* 'I fight, I conquer,' with a plural **wik-més.* This athematic present has been replaced by different forms in different languages: a thematic form with zero root vowel in OIr. *fichim,* 'I fight,' a present with infixed nasal in Lat. *uinco,* 'I conquer,' and a present with suffix **-ye-* in Lit. *veikiù,* 'I achieve' (*nu-veikiù,* 'I gain the victory'). In Germanic the representatives of **weikmi* are, on the one hand, the type Got. *weihan,* 'to fight,' made up of forms with vowel *e* and with the accent on the root as in **wéik-,* and, on the other hand, the type OI. *vega,* 'to beat,' derived from forms with no vowel and accent on the ending such as **wik´.* The OI. present *vega* has been treated as belonging to the type OI. *gefa,* 'to give,' with an original vowel in *-e-* without a sonant. Through contamination of the two types *wihan* and **wiyan,* we get, on the one hand, OE. *wigan,* 'to fight,' OS. *wigand,* and OHG. *wigant,* 'fighting,' and, on the other hand, OHG. *ubar-wehan,* 'to prevail over,' and Got. *and-waihan,* 'to resist.' Germanic offers several other examples of variations of this kind which can be explained in the same way.

In addition to presents with root vowels representing an ancient vowel *e,* which are the ordinary type, and presents with root vowel zero, which are exceptional and doubtlessly of secondary origin, there is a rather large number of forms with root vowel *a* in Germanic. These forms are of diverse origin; for the most part they replace ancient athematic forms. The present Got. *fara,* 'I drive' (in a vehicle) recalls the aorist Gr. *poreîn,* 'to procure.' The present Got. *mala,* 'I grind,' corresponds to Lit. *malù*; but OIr. *melim,* also of the thematic type, has another root vowel, and OSl. *meljǫ* has the root vowel *e* and a suffix **-ye-*; the combination represented by *meljǫ* replaces a stem with present **melə-, *molə-.*

Although the ancient type of thematic presents became the normal type of present for strong verbs, and although this type was considerably augmented, there are traces of other formations in Germanic. For example, the root IE. **prek-,* 'to ask, request,' which did not have a thematic root present in Indo-European, provided in Gothic a present with suffix **-ne-*: *fraihna,* 'I ask.' There is an appreciable number of forms with suffix **-ye-,* especially among the forms with Germanic root vowel *-a-*: Got. *hafjan,* 'to raise,' OI. *hefja,* and OHG. *heffan* (cf. Lat. *capiō,* 'I take'). From the root **sed-,* 'to sit,' we have, also with the suffix **-ye-,* OI. *sitja,* 'to sit,' OE. *sittan,* and OHG. *sizzan,* while Gothic shows the normal type *sitan,* 'to sit'; undoubtedly, neither form is of Indo-European date.

The present subjunctive of strong verbs is derived from the ancient optative of thematic presents: Got. *bairais,* 'that you may carry,' OHG. *berēs,* and Got. *bairai,* 'that he may carry,' OHG. *bere,* correspond exactly to the optatives Skr. *bhárēḥ,* 'you may carry,' *bháret,* 'he may carry,' and Gr. *phérois, phéroi.* Only the first-person singular presents some difficulty.

The imperatives Got. *bair* and OHG. *bir,* 'carry,' correspond exactly to Skr. *bhára* and Gr. *phére,* 'carry.' The finals have disappeared, and the forms in Germanic are reduced to roots without endings.

It is evidently in the strong verb that the habit of forming the infinitive from the stem of the present became fixed, for here is where this usage can be explained. The Germanic infinitive is based on an ancient type of abstract in *-ono-,* which had its counterpart in Indo-Iranian; for example, to Skr. *ádanam,* 'food,' compare Got. *itan,* 'to eat,' to Skr. *bháraṇam,* 'burden,' compare Got. *bairan,* 'to carry,' and so forth. These root nouns were found to be in agreement with presents such as Got. *ita,* 'I eat,' and *baira,* 'I carry.' A relationship was established between these nouns and these presents, and once it was established and the nouns in *-an* were considered as the infinitives of strong verbs of the usual type, it was possible to form an infinitive such as Got. *hafjan,* 'to raise,' from *hafja,* 'I raise,' and to do the same for all the verbs of the language. Old High German still inflected the infinitive, and we find forms like *berannes* (genitive) and *beranne* (dative). In Gothic and in Nordic there is no longer any trace of declension of the infinitive.

The preterite of strong verbs is based for the most part on the ancient type of Indo-European perfect. The Indo-European perfect was an athematic type, having special endings and presenting in the singular the prefinal vowel *o* but having no vowel in this position in the plural. Thus we have Skr. *véda,* 'I know,' and Gr. *(w)oîda,* but Skr. *vidmá,* 'we know,' and Gr. *(w)ídmen* (with displaced accent); for this verb, which has remained in Germanic with its perfect value, expressing the result obtained from the process,[2] we have Got. *wait,* 'I know,' and *witum,* 'we know.'

The perfect existed with or without reduplication. In Indo-Iranian and Greek the forms with redoubling are normal; we find therefore Skr. *riréca,* 'I have left,' and Gr. *léloipa.* In Germanic the forms without redoubling are the only ones in use in all the verbs where the present is

2. The process referred to here is that of *seeing.* The present from which Gr. *oida* is derived meant "I see." Hence *oida* literally meant "I have seen." The result is "I know."

based on a form with root vowel *e*, that is, in the usual type; thus we have Got. *laihw*, 'I have lent,' beside *leihwa*, 'I lend.' What characterizes the perfect in such a case is the vowel *a* (IE. *o*) in the singular and zero in the plural, with regard to the representative of the vowel *e* in the present. Thus we find in Gothic: *beitan*, 'to bite': *bait, bitum*; *bindan*, 'to bind': *band, bundum*; *giutan*, 'to pour': *gaut, gutum*; and so forth.

In the roots where the root vowel is followed by a single consonant, as in **wes-*, 'to remain, be,' and **bhèr-*, 'to carry,' it is not zero which marks the plural but *ē*. Thus in Gothic we have: *wisan*, 'to be': *was, wesum*; *giban*, 'to give': *gaf, gebum*; *bairan*, 'to carry': *bar, berum*; and so forth.

The use of this long vowel in forms of the preterite is not a specialty of Germanic; we find analogous examples notably in the Baltic languages and in Latin. In Latin for example, the perfect *sēdī*, 'I have been seated,' is opposed to the present *sĕdeō*, 'I am seated.'

It is also a long vowel, Germanic *ō*, which serves to characterize the entire preterite, singular and plural, of verbs which have Germanic *a* in the present. Thus we find in Gothic: *faran*, 'to drive' (a vehicle): *for, forum*.

In addition to the type without reduplication, Germanic has preserved traces of a perfect with reduplication in cases where the present has a special vowel arrangement which does not permit characterizing the perfect by the vowel, or where the vocalism is somehow outside the ordinary rules.

When the present has a vowel *a* before a sonant followed by a consonant, as in Got. *haitan*, 'to be named,' *stautan*, 'to jostle,' *haldan*, 'to hold,' and *fāhan* (from **fanhan*), 'to take,' the long *ō*, which exists only in an open syllable, is not usable. In this case, the preterite with reduplication is the rule: Got. *haihait, haihaitum*; *staistaut, staistautum*; *haihald, haihaldum*; and *faifāh, faifāhum*. In the same conditions Latin has the type *momordī*, 'I have bitten,' beside *mordeō*, 'I bite.' The same thing can be found in Irish. We also find a preterite with reduplication in cases where the present has a long vowel: thus Got. *slepan*, 'to sleep,' preterite *saizlep*, 'I fell asleep,' and *flokan*, 'to complain,' *faiflok*; and, with an alternation of vowel quality, Got. *letan*, 'to leave,' preterite *lailot*, and *saian*, 'to sow' (root **sē-*; cf. Lat. *sē-uī*, 'I have sown'), *saiso*.

The preterite with reduplication, which is based on an Indo-European type and which must have been a notable feature of common Germanic, is clearly preserved only in Gothic. It had the disadvantage of fitting poorly into the general system of the Germanic strong verb, where the root syllable always bears the initial accent and is thus placed in prominent position; by a unique exception, the root syllable of these preterites was found in an accent depression. The Northumbrian group of Old English dialects, which still kept the preterite with reduplication, shows this disadvantage: Got. *haihait* is paralleled by *heht*; Got. *lailot* by *leort* (with dissimilation of *l* to *r*); Got. *lailaik*, 'I have jumped,' by *leolc*; and so forth. The root element became unrecognizable. Under the action of the initial accent combined with the tendency toward dissimilation, the forms with reduplication have been replaced in Nordic and in the majority of Western dialects by forms which have a special vocalism, but which, like all the other forms of the strong verb, have the initial accent on the root syllable. Thus we have:

	Old Icelandic	Old English	Old High German
inf.	*heita*	*hātan*	*heizan* 'to be called'
pret.	*hēt*	*hēt*	*hiaz*
inf.	*halda*	*healdan*	*haltan* 'to hold'
pret.	*helt*	*heald*	*hialt*
inf.	(*h*)*laupa*	*hlēapan*	*loufan* 'to run'
pret.	(*h*)*liōþ*	*hlēop*	*liof*
inf.	*lāta*	*lāetan*	*lāzan* 'to leave'
pret.	*lēt*	*lēt*	*liaz*

Thus the preterites with reduplication were brought back to the general type of preterites of strong verbs. The general unity in the aspect of these forms, which common Germanic had not been able to bring about, was obtained in the course of the special development of the dialects.

The inflection of the perfect required special endings in Indo-European. In the plural, it would appear that the ancient secondary endings of the preterite had been generalized; we have in the third-person plural Got. *witun*, 'they know,' and *nemun*, 'they have taken,' where Germanic -*un* is based on *-*ṇt* (cf. Avestan -*at̯* of the secondary athematic type). The -*u*- of these forms was extended to the other persons of the plural, whence Got. *witum*, 'we know,' *nemum*, 'we have taken,' and *wituþ*, 'you know,' *nemuþ*, 'you have taken.' Old High German has *nāmum*, *nāmut*, and *nāmun*, and Old Icelandic has *nōmom*, *nōmod*, and *nōmo*. Thus for a type where the endings were added immediately to the root was substituted a type where, from the Germanic point of view, there is a vowel -*u*- between the root and the endings -*m*, -*d*, and -*nd*. The model of the present, where there was a vowel before the ending, as in the type Got. *bairam*, *bairiþ*, and *bairand*, had a good deal to do with this innovation.

In the singular, the situation was quite different. The ending in the first-person perfect was *-a*—Skr. *véda* and Gr. (*w*)*oida*, 'I know'—and that of the third person was *-e*—Skr. *véda* and Gr. (*w*)*oide*, 'he knows'; we also have OIr. *cechan*, 'I have sung,' from **kekana*, and *cechain*, 'he has sung,' from **kekane*. In Germanic, where the final vowels **-a* and **-e* disappeared before the most ancient texts were written, we find everywhere only forms without endings in the first and third persons: Got. *wait*, 'I know, he knows,' OI. *veit*, OE. *wāt*, and OHG. *weiz*. This treatment is of far-reaching importance from two points of view. Along with the imperative, it is the first case in which the Germanic forms are reduced to the root alone, without any visible ending. It is also the first case in which the forms for two different persons become identical and can no longer be distinguished by themselves. Other similar occurrences took place at various dates in the Germanic dialects, but this is the only one which is common to the whole group. The ambiguity of forms such as Got. *nam*, 'I have taken' and 'he has taken,' is therefore a highly significant fact.

Still to be considered is the second-person singular. The active ending of the Indo-European perfect began with a dental; it appears in Sanskrit as *-tha* and in Greek as *-tha*. Gothic and Scandinavian have kept it with the form *-t*. Germanic *-t* is the normal representative of an Indo-European **-th-* after a consonant and in cases like Got. *gaft*, 'you have given,' *tauht*, 'you have drawn,' and *wast*, 'you have been'; there was a restoration of *-t-* in a case like *waist*, 'you know,' where phonetically we should have **waiss*; and there is a pure and simple analogic extension based on the preceding examples in cases like *namt*, 'you have taken,' and *bart*, 'you have carried.' In Old Icelandic we find *veist*, 'you know' (which tends to be replaced by *veizt, veiz*).

As the analogic actions which it occasioned show, this second-person form caused difficulty because the ending began with a consonant. West Germanic avoided the difficulty by taking recourse to a quite different form for this second person, which did not belong to the perfect system. Let us take, for example, the verb which is in OE. *tēon*, OS. *tiohan*, and OHG. *ziohan*, 'to draw,' the third-person singular preterite of which is OE. *tēah*, OS. *tōh*, and OHG. *zōh*, and the third plural of which is OE. *tugon*, OS. *tugun*, and OHG. *zugun*. The second-person singular of this verb is OE. *tuge*, OS. *tugi*, and OHG. *zugi*. Here it is not a question of a perfect; we are facing the remainder of the thematic aorist of the Homeric Greek type *lípon*, 'I have left,' beside *leípō*, 'I leave,' and *leîpon*, 'I left.' This aorist was characterized by zero in the root vocalism and by the accent on the thematic vowel *e/o* (compare the Greek present participle *leípōn* with the aorist *lipōn*). Thus a form like OHG. *liwi*, 'you have lent,' beside *lēh,* 'I have lent, he has lent,' is to be compared with Homeric Greek *lipes* (where the accent is displaced). The maintenance of aorist forms in a Germanic dialect shows that common Germanic still had aorists. Common Germanic was more archaic in form than the oldest monuments of the Germanic languages, and the elimination of the archaisms took place largely in the course of the special history of the dialects. In OHG. *tōt,* 'he does, he acts,' there is still an old athematic present root which is even more archaic than a present such as Lat. *dat.*

Even in West Germanic a group has kept the ending of the perfect with its Germanic form *-t.* These are perfects which have not taken on the value of preterites, and which, having kept the old meaning of the Indo-European perfect, express the result obtained from a process: Old High German has *weist,* 'you know,' while Gothic has *waist;* and likewise it has *darft,* 'you need,' *gi-tarst,* 'you dare,' and *maht,* 'you can.' A preterite form could not indeed figure in what is called improperly the preterite-present, which is composed essentially of ancient perfects with the value of the present or of forms assimilated to perfects.

If we grant that the thematic aorist was maintained in common Germanic, it is possible that athematic aorists could also have been preserved. An inflection of the plural Got. *bitum, bituþ,* and *bitun* can be related to the athematic aorist Vedic *bhét,* 'he split,' participle *bhidán,* just as well as it can be related to an ancient perfect without reduplication. A mixture of perfects and of athematic aorists in the plural would explain the preterite meaning acquired as a general rule by the perfect in Germanic. However, we cannot state anything positively to this effect.

The Germanic preterite subjunctive was based on the type of perfect optative without reduplication or on an athematic aorist: the two forms could not be distinguished. The characteristic of the optative of all the Indo-European stems of the athematic type was **-yē-* in the singular and **-ī-* in the plural; this suffix was added to a stem with prefinal vocalism zero. Germanic generalized *-i-,* as we see in Got. second-person singular *bundeis,* third singular *bundi,* and in OHG. second-person singular *buntis,* third singular *bunti,* just as was the case in the plural first person Got. *bundeima* and OHG. *buntim.* The *-i-* of the athematic type had also been maintained in common Germanic in the athematic presents; Old High German still has for the verb "to be" the subjunctive second singular *sis,* third singular *si,* first plural *sim (sīn),* and so on (cf. Lat. *sīs, sit, simus*). Another present has preserved this type of subjunctive (ancient optative), but, because of the particular meaning of the verb, the optative serves as an indicative: opposite Lat. *uelis,* 'that you may wish,' *uelit,* 'that he may wish,' and *uelīmus,* 'that we may wish,' we find Got. *wileis, wili,* and *wileima,* and OHG. *wili* (2nd and 3rd sg.; the plural has another form in West Germanic); the original meaning is 'you would like, he would like, we should like.' The opposition of the present subjunctive of the type Got. *bindai* and of the preterite subjunctive of the type Got. *bundi* is secondary and became fixed in the course of the development of Germanic; the feeling for this opposition was so strong that the subjunctive of the verb "to be" became in Gothic *sijais, sijai, sijaima,* and so forth. In the preterito-presents, which like Got. *wait,* 'I know,' kept the inflection for the perfect with the meaning of the present, the subjunctive in *-i-* has persisted: Got. *wileis, wili, wileima,* and so on (cf. the type Skr. *vidyất,* 'he may know,' *vidyūh,* 'they may know').

The intransitive or passive past participle of strong verbs was formed with the aid of the Indo-European suffix *-no-*; the Germanic suffix is *-ana-,* derived from IE. *-ono-.* Beside presents of the ordinary type representing an Indo-European root vowel *e,* the vocalism for the past participle is in the zero degree; thus, opposite Got. *bindan,* 'to bind,' OI. *binda,* OE. *bindan,* and OHG. *bintan,* we have Got. *bundans,* OS. *gi-bundan,* OHG. *gi-buntan,* and OI. *bundenn,* OE. *bunden.* Slavic has *-enŭ:* OSl. *nesenŭ,* 'carried.' Gothic preserves a trace of IE. *-eno-* in the adjective *fulgins,* 'hidden,' opposite the infinitive *filhan,* 'to hide.' The long root vowel in the indicative plural and in the subjunctive of preterites like Got. *nam,* 'he took,' *bar,* 'he carried,' plurals *nēmun, bērun,* subjunctives *nēmī, bērī,* comes from aorist stems or from the present of athematic type. In the past participle the zero vocalism is obligatory: thus Got. *numans, baurans;* OHG. *ginoman, giboran;* OE. *numen, boren;* and OI. *numenn, borenn.*

The preterite-presents, which are very different, have the Indo-European suffix *-to-*; thus beside Got. *man,* 'I think,' and *munum,* 'we think,' we have *munds,* 'thought,' which corresponds exactly to Skr. *matdh* and Lat. *-mentus.* In most cases these participles were separated from the verbal system and treated as adjectives; thus, beside Got. *skal,* 'I owe,' and *skulum,* 'we owe,' we find Got. *skulds,* 'indebted, guilty.'

The preterite-presents, while keeping the inflection of the perfect, used the present participle; we find, for example, Got. *witands,* 'knowing,' and OHG. *wizzanti.* The ancient perfect participle either disappeared or was used apart from the verbal system; it is true that Gothic has kept the participle which corresponds to Gr. *(w)eid(w)ôs,* 'knowing,' but it uses it as a substantive: *weitwops,* 'witness.' Moreover, what has facilitated the extension of present participles to the preterite-presents is that certain of these forms are from ancient presents or have been contaminated by ancient presents. Thus Gothic *aih*, 'I possess,' is an ancient present (cf. Skr. *íçe*, 'I have power'); the *a* of the Got. *aih* represents not the *o* of a perfect but an initial *a-* placed before *i-* which occurs frequently in the ancient Indo-European languages, and this *a* is maintained in the plural: Got. *aigun*, OI. *eigo*, OE. *āgon*, and OHG. *eigun*. It is perhaps because we have here an ancient present that the past participle (become adjective) is in *-n-*: OI. *eigenn*, OE. *āgen*, OS. *ēgan*, OHG. *eigen*, 'own.' Therefore, the present participle Got. *aigands*, 'possessing,' is not surprising.

The present, the preterite, and the past participle, which together constitute the strong verb, belong, as we have seen, to three types which are of Indo-European date. The three forms have been placed in relation to one another so that on one of the three the others are formed when needed. Thus there are preterites formed secondarily from presents. For example, we have seen how the present Got. *winna* represents an ancient present *wenwō; on this present, a preterite *wann* and a past participle *wunnans* were formed. It would then be vain to try to explain directly each of the forms of a given strong verb; many of the forms one meets are explained by the system. This system, the general aspect of which is archaic, is composed largely of newly created forms. The divergences of detail which we observe among the dialects, in the second person of the preterite and in the numerous presents, show that if the ensemble of the system existed already in common Germanic, the detail was fixed only after the differentiation of the dialects.

The system of the strong verb was so well established, so balanced, so clear, and so consistent with the whole general plan of the language that it has been maintained in all of the Germanic languages. Even modern English has kept strong verbs with vocalic alternations. The group was enriched by new forms only rarely as when German borrowed the Lat. *scribere* and made of it the strong verb OHG. *skriban*. No doubt the verbs which constitute the group of strong verbs tend little by little to go out of use. Nevertheless, a language like German still has a very large number of strong verbs, with vocalic and even consonant alternations as in *ziehen, zog; sieden, sott; leiden, litt;* and so on.

C. Weak Verbs

The verbal formations known as "weak" all show common features: the present has a suffix; the preterite and the past participle have a common formation that is characterized by dental suffixes.

Unlike the strong verbs (other than the preterito-presents), the weak verbs have in the past participle the representative of the suffix IE. *-to-*, which figures in Lat. *monitus, amātus, finitus,* and so forth. This suffix had the form *-þa-*, which between vowels changed to *-da-* in all the weak verbs. Thus Gothic has *nasiþs,* 'saved,' fem. *nasida; salboþs,* 'anointed,' fem. *salboda;* and *habaiþs,* 'possessed,' fem. *habaida.* Old Icelandic has *safnaðr,* 'assembled,' *førðr* (from **fōridaR*), 'conducted,' and so on. Old English has *nered,* 'saved,' *dēmed,* 'judged,' and so on. Old High German has *gi-nerit,* 'saved,' *gi-salbōt,* 'anointed,' *gi-habēt,* 'possessed,' and so on.

The ancient voiceless pronunciation *-þa-* was maintained only in a few isolated verbs which form two groups. First there are verbs with presents in **-ye-*, in which the suffix of the past participle immediately follows a consonant and where the *-þa-* changed to *-ta-*: Got. *waurkjan,* 'to act,' participle *waurhts,* and similarly OI. *ortr,* OE. *ge-worht,* and OHG. *gi-worht;* Got. *bugjan,* 'to buy,' participle *bauhts,* and OE. *ge-boht;* Got. *þugkjan,* 'to seem,' participle *-þūhts,* and OI. *þōttr,* OE. *ge-dūht,* and OHG. *gi-dūht.* On the other hand, there are the preterite-presents; in the same conditions after a consonant the voiceless consonant is maintained as in Got. *þarf,* 'he has need,' *þaurfts,* 'necessary' (employed as an adjective); *mag,* 'I can,' *mahts;* and so forth. Beside *wait,* 'I know,' the Indo-European **wit-to,* 'known,' attested by Gr. *-wistos* for example, is represented by Got. *-wiss,* OI. *viss,* OE. *-wiss,* and OHG. *-wiss,* 'certain,' which became a simple adjective. The form *-þa-* was even maintained, beside *kann,* 'I know,' in Got. *kunþs* (fem. *kunþa*), OE. *kūd,* and OHG. *kund,* without any apparent reason for this unique anomaly.

Inasmuch as the Indo-European verb stems were entirely independent of one another, a derived verb always had a single stem, which was a present stem. The preterite stems of derived verbs which became the Germanic weak verbs are then of secondary creation, as are the formations of the same sort that we find in other languages. The origin of the form of the preterite of weak verbs in Germanic is not exactly known; it is not an Indo-European form, and consequently a comparison with other languages tells us nothing except that it is a new formation, posterior to the Indo-European period. At the time when the first monuments of Germanic appeared, the formation was entirely completed, so that a comparison of Germanic languages with one another does not teach us anything either. We encounter the same difficulty with the Latin perfectum of the type *amāui* and *monui,* about whose origin we can only form uncertain and precarious hypotheses.

The formation of the preterite of weak verbs is always parallel to that of the participle. Thus we find:

	Past Participle (nom. masc. sg.)	Preterite (1st pers. sg. ind.)
Germanic type in -*ō*-:		
Got.	*salboþs* (fem. *salboda*) 'anointed'	*salboda*
OHG.	*gi-salbōt*	*salbōta*
OI.	*kallaðr* 'called'	*kallaða*
Germanic type in -*i*-:		
Got.	*nasiþs* (fem. *nasida*) 'saved'	*nasida*
OHG.	*gi-nerit*	*nerita*
OI.	*talðr* 'said'	*talða*

When the participle has the form with the voiceless consonant -*þ*- or -*t*-, the preterite likewise has -*þ*- or -*t*-: for example, beside *kunþs*, 'known,' Gothic has *kunþa*, 'I knew,' and beside *waurhts*, 'accomplished,' it has *waurhta*, 'I accomplished.' The preterito-presents, which could not have a preterite based on the perfect since the ancient perfect furnished the form which acquired the value of a present, derived preterites from the past participle; for example, beside Got. *wait*, 'I know,' we have the preterite *wissa*, 'I knew, found out,' which is parallel to the ancient participle -*wiss*, 'known.'

The recent character of the formation of the weak preterite can be recognized by the disagreement of the inflection in the various Germanic languages:

Gothic	Old High German	Old Icelandic
salboda	*salbōta*	*kallaða*
salbodes	*salbōtōs*	*kallaðir*
salboda	*salbōta*	*kallaði*
salbodedum	*salbōtum*	*kallaðom*
salbodeduþ	*salbōtut*	*kallaðoð*
salbodedun	*salbōtun*	*kallaðo*

The Gothic form *salbodedum*, is instructive as to the origin of the preterite of weak verbs. Just as in Lat. *amābam*, 'I loved,' we think we recognize a type of infinitive *amā*- and an auxiliary meaning 'I was,' in the type Got. *salbo-dedum*, we believe we recognize an auxiliary, forms of the root IE. *dhē-, Germ. *dē-, for West Germanic attests the existence of a preterite with reduplication, the stem of which is *dē-d-: OHG. *tātum*, 'we made,' and OS. *dādun*. The forms of the singular such as Got. *salboda* and OHG. *salbota* seem to be derived from preterites without reduplication.

This would explain everything, and a detail of vowel structure supports this explanation. We have seen that the final has -*ē*- in the second-person singular in Got. *salbōdes* and OI. *kalladir*, and that it has -*ō*- in a part of West Germanic: OHG. *salbōtōs* and OS. *salbōdos* (beside *salbōdes*). Now, the root IE. **dhē-*, from which we have forms in -*ē*-, in the Armenian imperative aorist *di-r*, 'place,' for example, furnishes a present in -*ō*- in West Germanic: OE. *dōm*, OS. *dōm*, and OHG. (very ancient) *tōm*, 'I make.' The correspondence is striking.

If this hypothesis, which seems plausible, represents reality, we must admit that the weak preterites with characteristic voiceless consonant, such as Got. *waurhta*, 'I acted,' *kunþa*, 'I knew,' and so forth, acquired this voiceless consonant by analogy with the form of the past participle: in accordance with the model *salbōþs* (from **salbōdaz*) and *salboda*, and *munds*, 'thought,' and *munda*, 'I thought,' it was natural to form *waurhta* on *waurhts* and *kunþa* on *kunþs* (from **kunþaz*). This appears to be a good example of the power of innovation which characterizes Germanic.

The various types of weak verbs are distinguished by the form of the present and by the element which is found before the initial consonant of the endings for the past participles and preterites.

The most important type is the one in **-jan*, which has various origins. It is found principally in verbs derived from nouns, such as Got. *arbaidjan*, 'to work,' from *arbaiþs*, 'work,' and *dauþjan*, 'to kill,' from *dauþs*, 'death.' It is found also in causatives, such as *Got. satjan*, 'to seat,' opposite *sitan*, 'to sit'; *dragkjan*, 'to cause to drink,' opposite *drigkan*, 'to drink'; and so forth. The Indo-European causatives had the vowel *o* in the root (*a* in Germanic); the accent was on the suffix. In the causatives the opposition between the vowel of the causative and that of the original form to which it is opposed is a characteristic so important in the formation that for verbs which had the vowel *a* in the present, such as Got. *faran*, 'to go' (in a vehicle), *ō* was used to characterize the causative, as in Got. *forjan*, 'to drive' (a vehicle). This vocalism is ancient; Sanskrit, for example, has *pāráyati*, 'he causes to pass,' with *ā*, but Germanic has kept it only in the causatives which are opposed to presents with Germanic root vowel *a*.

The two formations, denominative and causative, are of ancient origin. The denominative Got. *namnjan*, 'to name' (OI. *nefna* and OHG. *nemnen*), from *namo*, 'name' (gen. sg. *namins*, nom. pl. *namna*), is formed like Gr. *onomaínō* (ancient **onomanyō*) from *ónoma*, 'name.' The causative Got. *-wardjan* (in *fra-wardjan*, 'to cause to perish'), beside *wairþan* (*fra-wairþan*, 'to perish'), corresponds to Skr. *vartáyati*, 'he causes to turn,' beside *vártati,* 'he turns,' and to OSl. *vratitŭ,* 'he causes to turn' (from **wortiti*). The Gothic form *-wardjan* shows both the root vowel and the ancient position of the accent.

The suffix for the present has two forms in Germanic, short *ĭ* or long *i,* depending on whether it is preceded by a single short syllable or by either a long syllable or two syllables; thus we have Got. *lagjan,* 'to spread, to put,' third singular *lagjiþ* (replacing **lagiþ*), and OHG. *leggan,* third singular *legit,* but Got. *sokjan,* 'to seek,' third singular *sokeiþ* and Got. *mikiljan,* 'to glorify' (from *mikils,* 'great'), third singular *mikileiþ,* 'he glorifies.' The two forms in *-ĭ-* and *-i-* are both ancient, and Latin distributes them in much the same way as Germanic; on the one hand it has *capis,* 'you take' (1st pers. *capiō*), which is the exact correspondent of OHG. *hevis* (Got. *hafjis* has *j* after the 1st pers. *hafja*), and on the other hand it has *sāgis,* 'you go after' (1st pers. *sāgiō*), which is the exact correspondent of Got. *sokeis,* and it also has *sepelis,* 'you bury.' The only divergence between Germanic and Latin is in the first-person plural, which has the thematic vowel in Germanic: we find *hafjam* and *sokjam* in Gothic, while Latin has, without the thematic vowel, *capimus* and *sāgimus.* It is Germanic which keeps here the ancient state of things, as can be shown by a comparison with Albanian.

Parallel to the causative presents, there was in Indo-European a special form of adjective in **-to-* with the root vowel of the causatives and an *-i-* before the suffix, as in Skr. *vartitáḥ,* beside *vartáyati* (Latin has *monitus,* 'forewarned,' beside *moneō,* 'I warn,' that is, 'I cause to think'). It is to Skr. *vartitáḥ* that Got. *-wardiþs* corresponds, and it is after the common Germanic form **wardidaz,* 'which has been caused to turn,' that the preterite, Got. *-wardida,* has been constructed. On this model, an ancient one for the causatives, the type of weak verbs in *-jan* was formed; we also have *dauþida,* 'I killed,' *sokida,* 'I sought,' and so on. This system results from a Germanic arrangement.

In addition to the denominatives and causatives already mentioned, the verbs in **-jan* include types of presents in which a suffix **-ye/o-* has been directly added to the root, as in Got. *huljan,* 'to hide' (beside the root verb OHG. *helan,* 'to hide') or *sokjan,* 'to seek' (cf. Lat. *sāgiō*). They have all been fused by Germanic into a single type.

Most verbs in **-jan* have conformed to the types of *lagjan* and *-wardjan*; however, some ancient root verbs have kept a preterite of the strong type, and thus opposite *hafja,* 'I raise,' Gothic has the preterite *hof* and the participle *hafans.* Moreover, not all the verbs had the *-i-*; opposite the present Got. *þagkja,* 'I think,' which corresponds to Old Lat. *tongeō,* 'I think,' we find the preterite *þāhta* and the participle *þāhts,* and opposite

Got. *þugkjan,* 'to seem,' we have the preterite *þūhta* and the participle -*þūhts.* It is a form such as Got. *þāhta,* namely *brāhta* which serves as the preterite for Got. *briggan,* 'to bring.'

The type of weak verbs in *-*ōn* is parallel to the Latin type in -*ā*-, that of *amāre,* 'to love.' This group is composed essentially of verbs derived from nouns like Got. *fiskon* and OHG. *fiscōn,* 'to fish,' from Got. *fisks* and OHG. *fisc,* 'fish.' The past participle and the preterite, Got. *fiskoþs* and *fiskoda,* are formed like *amātus* and *amāui* of the corresponding Latin type. The Germanic inflection of the type in *-*ōn* is exactly parallel to that of the Latin type in -*āre;* Got. *salbo, salbos,* and so forth behave like Lat. *amō, amās,* and so forth.

The type in *-*ēn* is more obscure. It often corresponds to that of Latin verbs in -*ēre* which, like *tacēre,* 'to be silent,' express a state; and, indeed, OHG. *dagēn* corresponds exactly to Lat. *tacēre.* However, it is for the most part only in Old High German that this type is distinct, and that we have *dagēm, dagēs, dagēt,* and so on, with *dagēta* in the preterite. Except in the first-person singular, the German inflection corresponds exactly to that of the type of Lat. *tacēre,* and OHG. *dagēs* is the perfect correspondent of Lat. *tacēs.* In all the other Germanic languages the type presents obscurities. For example, parallel to OHG. *habēm,* 'I have,' which is a verb expressing the state of someone 'who holds,' and which is of the same root as Got. *hafjan,* OI. *hefja,* and OHG. *heffan,* 'to raise' (cf. Lat. *capiō,* 'I take'), the Gothic inflection is *haba,* 'I have,' *habais, habaiþ,* with forms in -*ai*- where the type in -*jan* has forms in -*i*- or -*ī*-. Consequently, we find *habais,* 'you have,' just as we have *hafjis,* 'you take' (replacing **hafis*), and *sokeis,* 'you seek'; the infinitive is *haban* and the preterite *habaida.* In Old Saxon there are some forms with a Germanic suffix -*ja*-: infinitive *hebbian* and present *hebbia,* beside second singular *habes.* Likewise in Old English we find the infinitive *habban,* 'to have,' and first singular *haebbe,* 'I have,' beside *hafas(t),* 'you have.' In Old Icelandic these diverse forms are peculiar to certain verbs; the first-person singular present of *hafa,* 'to have,' is *hefe,* 'I have.' The type in -*ē*- has then in Germanic very diverse forms in the different dialects.

The type in *-nan,* which indicates the beginning of an action, was also not developed in all branches of Germanic. It is well represented in Gothic, as in *ga-waknan,* 'to wake up,' and *fullnan,* 'to fill up,' and in Old Icelandic, as in *vakna,* 'to wake up.' In Gothic the inflection is the same as in the strong type *bindan*—for example, *ga-wakna, ga-waknis,* and so on;

but the preterite has -*o*-, as in the type *salbon*—for example, *ga-waknoda*, 'I woke up.' In Old Icelandic the inflection is entirely that of the type in -*o*-: *vakna, vaknar*, like *kalla*, 'I call,' *kallar*. In West Germanic we find only traces of this type in -*n*-.

The general category of weak verbs with a dental in the suffix of the past participle and the preterite was then already constituted in common Germanic. The special types, however, were not yet fixed and were established only during the development of the different dialects. Moreover, the various types did not maintain clear distinctions in the later development of the dialects. The characteristics of each type were obscured by the general alteration of the unaccented vowels. The modern Germanic languages oppose only one type of weak verbs to what remains of the strong verbs.

D. Personal Inflection

Personal inflection was very complicated in Indo-European. Common Germanic kept this complexity, but very soon a tendency toward simplification became evident

The double series of active and middle endings, of which Gothic still has important vestiges in the present, was simplified in West Germanic and in Nordic by the elimination of the whole middle series.

The opposition of the present and the imperfect by means of endings called "primary" and "secondary" disappears. The so-called present stem no longer has more than one inflection which serves to express both the present and the future. The contrast of Vedic *bhárāmi* and Gr. *phérō*, 'I carry,' with Vedic *bháram* and Homeric Greek *phéron*, 'I was carrying,' no longer exists in Germanic, not even in traces.

The preterite preserves a mixture of Indo-European endings for the preterite and the aorist, as we have seen (p. 77ff.).

There are then two inflections, one for the present, the other for the preterite. This difference in inflection is added to the difference in stems; it is not sufficient in itself as it was in Indo-European.

In addition, the alteration of finals diminished the importance of endings, and the language was led to react by amplifying the endings. Extensive confusion of personal forms tended to occur. Thus the personal inflection became disturbed and tended to disappear.

With the exception of the dual, which was maintained only in Gothic (in the first and second persons, not in the third) and in runic Norse, the finals for the present are as follows for the strong verb *bindan*, 'to bind';

these examples will give a sufficient idea of the whole inflection of the present:

Got.	OI.	OE.	OS.	OHG.
binda	*bind*	*binde*	*bindu*	*bintu*
bindis		*bindes(t)*	*bindis*	*bintis*
bindiþ	*bindr*	*binded*	*bindid*	*bintit*
bindam	*bindom*			*bintamēs*
bindiþ	*binded*	*bindad*	*bindad*	*bintet (bintat)*
bindand	*binda*			*bintant*

The final of Got. *binda*, 'I bind,' OS. *bindu*, and so forth represents phonetically the Indo-European -*ō* of the Greek type *phérō* (see above, p. 47).

The final -*is* (in West Germanic) or *-iz* (from which we have -*r* in Scandinavian) corresponds to the Sanskrit type in -*asi* of *bhárasi*, IE. *-esi*. The difference between *-iz* and *-is* cannot be explained because we do not know the principle of the distribution of *s* and *z* in such a position.

The final *-id*/*-iþ* of the third singular corresponds to Skr. -*ati*, Old Russian -*eti*, and IE. *-eti*; it is preserved in Gothic (where the ancient -*id* changed phonetically to -*iþ* but persists sometimes before a vowel: *gibid imma*, 'he gives to him'), in runic Norse (*bariutiþ*, 'he breaks'), and in West Germanic. Scandinavian early replaced the form for the third person with that of the second, whence *bindr*, 'you bind, he binds.'

The first-person plural of the type Got. *bindam* and OI. *bindom* corresponds to a type without final fricative, with or without a final nasal like Ionic-Attic *phéromen*; it does not tally with Skr. -*āmaḥ* or Lat. -*imus*. The OHG. *bintamēs* is a type of obscure origin.

The second-person plural of the type Got. *bindiþ* and so on corresponds to the type Skr. *bháratha*, Gr. *phérete*, and OSl. *berete*, 'you carry,' and the third-person plural of the type Got. *bindand*, OI. *binda*, and OHG. *bintant* corresponds to the type Skr. *bhdranti*, 'they carry,' Doric Greek *phéronti*, and Lat. *ferunt*.

The very surprising use of the second-person singular for the third in Scandinavian and of the third plural for the first and second in Old English and in Old Saxon shows to what extent the personal inflection tends to become confused in Germanic; in Old English and Old Saxon the verbal inflection includes only one form for the three persons of the plural. In Gothic the medio-passive inflection, which still existed, used the form of the third singular also for the first, *bairada*, 'I am carried, he is carried,' and the form of the third plural also for the first and the second, *bairanda*, signifying 'we are carried, you are carried, they are carried.'

Phonetic changes contributed to the confusion. Thus the change of -*m* final to -*n* in German caused *zugum*, 'we have drawn,' to become *zugun*, and this became confused with *zugun*, 'they have drawn.'

From that time it became the custom to indicate person by the use of the personal pronoun. The unaccented forms of the personal pronoun, which were added to verb forms and fused with them, then played an important role. Thus, in Nordic, *ek*, 'I,' and *þu*, 'you,' were placed after the verb so that we find, for example, OI. *em-k*, 'I am,' *es-tu* and *es-t*, 'you are.' In Old High German *bindis*, 'you bind,' was replaced very soon by *bindis-t(u)*, and it is this form which became fixed; likewise, in Old English *bindes* tended to be replaced by *bindes-t*, where -*t* represents -*þ* changed to -*t* after -*s*. This procedure is far away from the Indo-European type in which each grammatical form sufficed unto itself.

Chapter X

The Noun

A. *Generalities*

NOMINAL INFLECTION tended to become simplified like verbal inflection.

The nominal forms for the dual number disappeared. From the time of the most ancient monuments in all of the dialects the only trace left is in the personal pronoun.

An Indo-European noun was always presented in a special case form. The number of cases was eight: nominative, accusative, vocative, genitive, ablative, locative, dative, and instrumental. No Germanic language distinguishes the ablative, the dative, and the locative, a single form being used for all three. The instrumental also lost almost all of its special marking and what was expressed by the instrumental tended to receive the common form of the dative-ablative-locative; however, West Germanic still had at an ancient date vestiges of the instrumental. The nominative, the accusative, the genitive, the dative (locative-ablative), and the vocative constituted distinct categories in common Germanic; but the vocative was distinct from the nominative only in the singular, and then only in some of the forms. The nominative and the accusative often had the same form.

The Indo-European noun distinguished three genders in quite different ways. The neuter was distinguished from the masculine only in three cases: nominative, accusative, and vocative, all the other case forms being identical with those of the masculine. This state of things persisted in Germanic where the neuter remained distinct in these three cases only.

A feminine noun was distinguished in Indo-European from a masculine noun or a neuter noun by the fact that the adjective modifying it had a special stem in the feminine: a substantive was masculine or neuter in Greek if it was modified by an adjective in -*o*-, such as Gr. *néos*, 'new' (neuter, *néon*); it was feminine if it was modified by an adjective in -*ā*-, such as Gr. *néā*. This distinction was maintained in Germanic, but it reacted on the substantive: where Indo-European had feminine substantives in -*o*- such as Gr. *nyós*, 'daughter-in-law,' Germanic eliminated these and feminized the corresponding forms: OE. *snuru*, OHG. *snur* (and *snura*), and OI. *snor* changed to the type in -*ā*-. Inversely, Indo-European had stems in -*ā*- which were masculine, such as Lat. *scriba*, 'the one who writes'; Germanic has nothing comparable. Germanic distinguishes then in the substantive masculine or neuter stems like those in -*a*- (IE. *-*o*-) and feminine stems like those in -*ō*- (IE. *-*ā*-); and, generally speaking, the distinction of the masculine from the feminine was marked most often in the form itself. This is an innovation which is not peculiar to Germanic, but which separates Germanic from the Indo-European type.

Indo-European nouns were inflected in different ways depending on the ending of the stem. The stems in *-*e*/*o*, called thematic, had an inflection quite different from that of the stems in *-*ā*-; and the stems ending in a consonant or a sonant (**y*, *w*, *r*, *l*, *m*, *n*), while having numerous common traits, showed divergences among themselves. Common Germanic kept the principal features of this system while tending to simplify it by changing consonant stems to vocalic types (as we have seen on p. 64), or by eliminating words of this type, which, being anomalous, easily go out of use.

However, Germanic presents here a singular innovation which has no equivalent in any other language. While everywhere types of stems ending in sonants like *r* and *n* progressively lose their importance, Germanic freely developed the type in -*n*-. Stems in -*n*- were doubtlessly numerous in Indo-European, and the ancient languages like Sanskrit, Greek, and Latin still have many of them; even greatly altered languages like Armenian have many stems in -*n*-. However, no language made of the type in -*n*- one of the most productive types of new forms. Normally, we shall see, Germanic adjectives had two forms: one, called strong, was subjected to the influence of the demonstratives; the other, called weak, was a form in -*n*-. A great number of masculine, neuter, and feminine nouns received a suffix *-*en*-/*-on*-/*-n*-; thus the neuter noun for "heart" appeared not as a stem without a suffix like Lat. *cor, cordis*, but as a stem in -*n*-: Got. *hairto*, gen. *hairtins*. A masculine word from the language of childhood, *atta*, 'papa' (cf. Gr. *átta* and Lat. *atta*), was inflected in Gothic *atta*, gen. *attins*. The feminine word for "woman," IE. *g^wenā* (OSl. *žena*), is in Gothic *qino*, gen. *qinons*. Examples of this sort could be multiplied. The types in -*n*-, masculine, neuter, and feminine, are normal types; and the change to the inflection in -*n*- is a means of rendering normal a word of a formerly anomalous type, like the word *g^wenā*, 'woman,' or an unusual word ending in -*a*, like the children's word *atta*, or a stem ending in an occlusive, like the word for "heart," *kerd*-, from which we have Got. *hairto*.

A language like German, which has kept up to the present a considerable amount of case inflection, still has a recognizable nominal inflection in -n.

B. The Substantives

Between Indo-European and common Germanic the type of inflection changed profoundly, as we have seen. Furthermore, the number of case forms was reduced, and the finals were increasingly altered. Yet, aside from these general changes and these general tendencies to change, common Germanic remained faithful to the old Indo-European usages, and the forms which we encounter in the ancient Germanic dialects, while having a new aspect, perpetuate for the most part Indo-European forms.

Let us take, for example, the inflection of Indo-European stems in *-e/o-*, which in Indo-European included masculines, feminines, and neuters but which no longer included feminines in Germanic. The inflection of these stems took on a new character in Germanic because the alternation *e/a* was no longer perceptible as such, because in some of the forms the vowels *e/a* even tended to disappear, and, finally, because the endings fused with the vowel of the stem in a final which characterized each case. Nevertheless, nearly all the forms reproduced ancient Indo-European forms.

The forms of the singular were all ancient.

The masculine-feminine Indo-European nominative in *-os* (Skr. -*aḥ*, Gr. -*os*, OLat. -*os*, Lit. -*as*) changed to *-az*, which is represented in old runic Norse by -*aR*. The vowel *-a-* then disappeared in all of the dialects, as did the *-z* final in West Germanic, so that we have Got. *dags*, 'day,' OI. *dagr*, OE. *dæg*, OS. *dag*, and OHG. *tag* (see above, p. 6).

The masculine-feminine Indo-European accusative, for which the finals are -*am* in Sanskrit, -*om* in Old Latin, and -*on* in Greek, -*an* in Old Prussian, was in *-an*, from which we have -*a* in common Germanic; this -*a* is still found in old runic Norse. Then the -*a* disappeared, and we have everywhere only Got., OI., and OS. *dag*, OE. *dæg*, and OHG. *tag*. The forms for the nominative and the accusative were thus confused in West Germanic by the simple play of phonetic changes.

The vocative was in *-e* in Indo-European: Skr. -*a*, Gr. -*e*, Lat. -*e*, and OSl. -*e*. This final vowel disappeared, and Gothic has *dag* in the vocative. In Nordic the vocative no longer had a form distinct from the nominative, following the analogy of the plural and some other types in the singular, which had already lost this distinction. In West Germanic the confusion of the nominative singular and the vocative singular was produced phonetically.

To the nominative-accusative neuter Sanskrit in *-am*, Old Latin in *-om* and Greek in *-on*, Old Prussian in *-an*, Germanic corresponds in runic Norse with *-a*; then this *-a* disappeared, and, opposite Skr. *yugám*, 'yoke,' Gr. *zdygón*, and Lat. *iugum*, we have Got *juk*, OI. *ok*, OE. *geoc*, and OHG. *joch*.

The genitive of these stems is in the form *-is* in Gothic, *-s* in Scandinavian, and *-es* and *-as* in West Germanic. The genitive of stems in *-e/o-* is a form with characteristics varying from one Indo-European language to another: the type Lat. *lupī* has nothing in common with the type Lit. *vilko* or OSl. *vlĭka*, 'of the wolf,' and the latter have nothing in common with the types Skr. *vŕkasya*, Homeric Gr. *lykoio*, and so forth. The Germanic forms are based on *-e-so* and *-o-so*, from which we have on the one hand Got. *-is* (*wulfis*, 'of the wolf') and OE., OS., and OHG. *-es* (OHG. *wolfes*), and on the other hand old runic Norse *-as* (OI. *-s*), Northumbrian OE. *-æs*, and OS. *-as*. The final *-so* attested in Germanic is ancient; it is found notably in the interrogative OSl. *če-so*, 'of what.'

The form called dative in Gothic, Scandinavian, and Old English serves as the dative, locative, ablative, and instrumental. It is therefore difficult to determine its origin, which is ambiguous. In Old Saxon and in Old High German an "instrumental," OS. *dagu* and OHG. *tagu*, is distinguished from the "dative," OS. *dage* and OHG. *tage*. The Got. *daga* may correspond both to OS. *dagu* and to OS. *dage* in form.

In the plural, the forms are to some extent less clear than in the singular. However, the accusative plural in *-ans* of Gothic, *dagans*, represents exactly an Indo-European type and corresponds to Cretan Gr. *-ons* and Old Prussian *-ans*, which still give an exact idea of Indo-European usage. The nominative-accusative neuter plural of Got. *waurda*, OI. *bǫrn*, 'children' (from *barnu*), OE. *hofu*, 'course,' and OS. *grabu*, 'graves,' corresponds to the Vedic type in *-ā*, the Slavic type in *-a*, and so on.

The dative plural with Gothic *-am*, Old Icelandic *-om*, and West Germanic *-um* represents the vowel *-o-* followed by an ending with initial *m*; in fact, as in Slavic and Baltic, Germanic uses in the dative plural a form beginning with *-m-*, while Indo-Iranian, Italic, Celtic, and others have representatives of a form with *-bh-*: Skr. *-bhyaḥ*, Lat. *-bus*, and so forth.

In the stems in *-ā-*, the nominative singular in *-ā* (cf. Skr. *-ā* and Gr. *-ā*) and the accusative singular in *-ān* (cf. Skr. *-ām* and Gr. *-ān*) became confused in Gothic and German: nom.-acc. sg. Got. *giba*, 'gift,' OS.

geba, and OHG. *geba*. A difference was maintained in Old English: nom. *giefu*, acc. *giefe*. Such a distinction also existed in very ancient Nordic but soon disappeared. In the plural, the nominative and the accusative both had the final *-ās* (Skr. *-āh*) in Indo-European; and in all branches of Germanic the two cases are merged: Got. *-os*, OI. *-ar*, OE. and OS. *-a*, and OHG. *-ā*.

The stems in *-i-* kept in common Germanic a distinctive inflection. However, we find some alteration of this inflection at an early date. In the nominative the ancient final was *-is* (cf. Skr. *-ih*, Gr. *-is*, and Lit. *-is*), which became *-iz* in Germanic; *-iR* is attested in runic Norse, and opposite OSl. *gosti*, 'guest,' and Lat. *hostis*, 'stranger, enemy,' we have runic Norse *-gastiR*. But the *i* disappeared early in the nominative and accusative so that we have in Gothic, nom. *gasts*, 'guest,' and acc. *gast*; in Old Saxon and Old High German, nom.-acc. *gast*; and in Old Icelandic, nom. *gestr* and acc. *gest*—that is, forms which agree perfectly with those of the type Got. *dags*, 'day.' In each Germanic language the genitive and dative singular of all the masculines in *-i-* changed independently to the type of Germanic stems in *-a-*, as in Got. gen. *gastis*, dat. *gasta*; OHG. gen. *gastes*, dat. *gaste*; and so on. The feminines alone preserved in the singular the ancient type in *-i-*: Got. gen. *anstais*, 'of the load,' dat. *anstai*; OHG. gen.-dat. *ensti*. In the plural the inflection remained entirely distinct; thus we have Got. nom. *gasteis*, 'guests,' acc. *gastins*, and dat. *gastim*.

The type in *-u-* was preserved more clearly because the vowel *u* ordinarily persisted better than *i*. The nominative and the accusative corresponding to Skr. *sūnúh*, 'son,' *sūnúm* and to Lit. *sūnùs*, *súnų* are in runic Norse *sunuR*, *sunu*, as we expect; Gothic has *sunus*, *sunu*, and the oldest High German has nom.-acc. *sunu*, as do Old English and Old Saxon. Likewise, in the nominative-accusative singular neuter, parallel to Vedic *páçu*, 'herd,' and Lat. *pecu*, we have Got. *faihu*, OS. *fehu*, and OHG. *fihu*, 'herd, wealth.' The inflection of the other cases, parallel to those with stems in *-i-*, is quite distinctive as in Gothic gen. sg. *sunaus* and dat. *sunau*. In the nominative plural, a form like Got. *sunjus* represents, element by element, IE. *sunewes* and corresponds to the type Skr. *sūnávah*, 'sons,' and OSl. *synove* (cf. Gr. *-e(w)es* in the nominative plural masculine of stems in *-u-*).

Stems originally ending in an occlusive presented complications in treatment which provoked the elimination of the type. Some, however, preserved certain special forms. Thus, parallel to Lat. *nox*, 'night,' gen.

noctis, we find in the singular Got. nom. *nahts,* acc. *naht* (ancient **nahtu*), gen. *nahts,* and dat. *naht*; in Old High German a single form, *naht,* corresponds to all these Gothic forms so that *naht* serves for all the cases of the singular.

The stems in *-n-* kept separate inflections which differed according to gender. The masculines and neuters still had curious vestiges of vocalic alternations. Thus, in the masculine we find in Gothic the nom. sg. *hana,* 'cock,' and acc. *hanan* (from **-hananu*), but gen. *hanins* and dat. *hanin*; in Old High German, we find nom. *hano* and acc. *hanun,* but gen. *hanen* and dat. *hanin.* These are old vocalic alternations which serve to distinguish the accusative from the genitive and the dative. In the neuter we have in Gothic nom.-acc. sg. *hairto,* 'heart,' gen. *hairtins,* dat. *hairtin,* and nom.-acc. pl. *hairtona,* gen. *hairtane*; in Old High German we find nom.-acc. sg. *herza,* gen. *herzen,* dat. *herzin.* The feminines, which are generally of secondary formation, do not have vocalic alternations; thus, in the singular we have in Gothic nom. *qino,* 'woman,' acc. *qinon,* gen. *qinons,* and dat. *qinon.* Except in the nominative singular, which has special forms, the nasal is well preserved in the whole inflection. However, in the dative plural, where the ending begins with *-m-,* the *n* of the stem has everywhere been eliminated before the *m* of the ending; thus we have Got. *hanam,* 'for the cocks,' *hairtam,* 'for the hearts,' and *qinom,* 'for the women'; this is the case in all of the dialects.

Thus, in common Germanic the variety of Indo-European types still existed almost in its entirety. Nevertheless, from the time of the most ancient texts, the dialects tended to restrict this variety. The ancient texts still show many traces, which the alteration of finals rapidly effaced. By the time of the Middle Ages, we find that inflections either become unified or they disappear. Of all the case characteristics of the singular, English has kept only the *-s* of the genitive OE. *dæges.* However, since relations between words in modern English are indicated not by inflections but by particles, *-s* has the effect of a particle, although it is less autonomous than a preposition like *of*; and, since all words in the language behave according to the same pattern, *-s* can be used with any word regardless of whether it belonged to the type of OE. *dæg.* While a remainder of the ancient case inflection has survived in English, we can see that it has changed character. As for the form, the *-s* which marks possession in English is a remnant of the *s* of the type OE. *dæges*; with regard to the role played by this element, which bears upon a whole nominal phrase, we are in the presence of a new linguistic structure.

Even in German, where the ancient character of the language has survived in some degree, the old forms have often acquired new values. Thus,
Indo-European had stems in *-es-*, for example in the word represented by
Skr. *rájaḥ*, 'dark space,' gen. *rájas-aḥ*, and by Gr. *érebos*, 'dark region,' gen.
erébeos (from **erebes-os*). The Gothic correspondent, *riqis*, 'darkness,'
became similar to the type *yuk* and formed a genitive *riqizis*. Old High
German kept nouns of this sort, but the ancient *-es-* appeared only in the
plural in the form *-ir-*, representing **-iz-*; thus we have *kalb*, 'calf,' gen.
sg. *kalbes*, but in the plural we have *kelbir*, gen. *kelbiro*. Hence it comes about
that *-ir*, which represents the Indo-European suffix **-es-*, has the effect of
a plural characteristic; modern German, opposing *kälber*, 'calves,' to
kalb, 'calf,' uses the ancient suffixal element *-er* as a plural ending and
employs it in many words which never had stems in **es-*.

Thus, the modern Germanic languages—even the least innovating
among them—are far away from the Indo-European type which common
Germanic still maintained in several of its aspects.

C. The Adjective

The adjective did not have its own inflection in Indo-European. Its only
particularity consisted in its having two stems, one for the masculine-
neuter, as in **newo-*, 'new' (nom. sg. Skr. *návaḥ*, Gr. *néos*, Lat. *nouos*, and
OSl. *novŭ*), the other for the feminine, as in **newā-*, 'new' (nom. sg. Skr.
návā, Gr. *néā*, Lat. *noua*, and OSl. *nova*). The masculine-neuter stem permitted two inflections, one for the masculine (nom. sg. Skr. *návaḥ*, Gr.
néos, Lat. *nouos*, and OSl. *novŭ*), the other for the neuter (nom.-acc. sg.
Skr. *návam*, Gr. *néon*, Lat. *nouom*, and OSl. *novo*). Each of the adjective
stems was inflected like those of the substantives of the same type.

On the other hand, the demonstrative, the interrogative-indefinite, and
adjectives signifying "one," "all," "same," and the like had special
inflections in most cases. In the masculine-neuter they were in general
stems in *-e/o-*, in the feminine they were stems in *-ā-*. However, many of
the cases had finals which were unlike those for substantives and ordinary
adjectives. For example, comparable to the nominative-accusative neuter
type Skr. *návam*, Gr. *néon*, and Lat. *nouom*, we have the demonstrative Skr.
tát, 'this,' Gr. *tó* (ancient **tót*), and Lat. *is-tud*, which has a special
characteristic.

Germanic faithfully preserved the peculiarities of the inflection of the
demonstrative type; it even further developed them.

An archaism as strange as the use in the nominative masculine and
feminine singular for the demonstrative **te/o-*, **tā-* of a form belonging to

another root was maintained: we find masc. Got. *sa*, OI. *sā* (and OE. *sē*), opposite Skr. *sá* and Gr. *ho*; and we also find fem. Got. *so*, OI. *sū* (and OE. *sēa*), opposite Skr. *sá* and Doric Gr. *há*. The German group alone reacted, and we find in the masculine OS. *thē*, *thie* and OHG. *der*; in the feminine we find OS. *thiu*, *thia* and OHG. *diu*.

The dative masculine-neuter singular Got. *þamma* corresponds to the type Skr. *tásmai* (dative), *tásmāt* (ablative), *tásmin* (locative), and to Old Prussian *stesmu*, 'to this one,' *kasmu*, 'to whom'; the forms of the other dialects, OS. *themu* and OHG. *demu* on the one hand and OI. *þeim* and OE. *dǣm* on the other, have undergone alterations but still belong to the same type.

In the feminine we find the gen. sg. Got. *þizos*, OS. *thera*, and OHG. *dera* and the dat. Got. *þizai*, OS. *theru*, and OHG. *deru*. These forms are of a type comparable to Skr. *tásyāḥ*, *tásyai* and to the dative Old Prussian *stessiei*. The forms OI. *þeirrar*, *þeirre* and OE. *daēre* represent a secondary alteration of the ancient type.

The accusative singular, for which the demonstrative used the same ending as the substantive, received secondarily its own form. The special form, OI. *þann* and OHG. *den* of the accusative masculine singular, opposite Skr. *tám* and Gr. *tón*, results from the maintenance of the final nasal in this monosyllabic form, while it disappeared in the polysyllables. The monosyllable was avoided by the addition of a particle in Got. *þan-a*, OE. *don-e*, and OS. *then-a*. Thus the accusative of the demonstratives took on an aspect different from that of the substantives.

In the nominative plural masculine, only Germanic and Indo-Iranian preserved the Indo-European state of things. The form of the nominative Got. *þai*, OE. *dā*, OS. *thē*, and OHG. *dē* (as well as old runic Norse *þai-R*, with the addition of *-R* as in the substantives, from which we have OI. *þeir*) is opposed to the form of the substantives (Got. *-os*, and so on), just as Skr. *té*, 'these,' is opposed to the Sanskrit form in *-āḥ* of the nominative plural of stems in *-ă-*.

In the dative and genitive plurals, the masculine-neuter and the feminine are not differentiated: dat. Got. *þaim*, OI. *þeim*, OE. *dǣem*, OS. *thēm*, and OHG. *dēm* (cf. OSl. dat. *těmŭ*, instrumental *těmi*, and, with endings in initial *-bh-*, Skr. Vedic dat. *tébhyaḥ*, instrumental *tébhiḥ*); gen. OI. *þeirra*, OE. *dāra*, and, with alteration, Got. *þize* and *þizo*, OS. *thero*, and OHG. *dero* (cf. OSl. *těxŭ* and Skr. *téṣām*).

The inflection of the "demonstrative" type served in Indo-European for adjectives signifying "one," "all," "same," and "other" and for a few additional ones having analogous meanings. This permitted a more widespread action of the inflection of the "demonstrative" type. Forms of this type developed for all the stems in -*o*- in Greek, Latin, Irish, and Slavic. In Lithuanian the inflection of the "demonstrative" type was adopted for all adjectives, which thus found themselves with an inflection different from that of the substantives; from that time, the substantives remained unharmed by any action of the demonstratives and the assimilated adjectives. A comparable occurrence took place in Germanic where the adjectives also acquired the inflection of the demonstrative type and, consequently, had forms different from those of the substantives in most of the cases. The point of departure for this differentiation of adjectives and substantives is found no doubt in the nominative plural: the final for the masculine was originally *-*ōs*, and for the feminine it was *-*ās*; these two finals were merged in Germanic, where *ō* and *ā* both became *ō*; the introduction of *-*ai* of the demonstratives into the nominative plural masculine of adjectives re-established the distinction, as we see in Gothic masc. *blindai*, 'blind,' and fem. *blindos*.

The principle of the extension of the inflection of the "demonstrative" type to all adjectives is of common Germanic date, but the extension was not completed, at least for some of the cases, until the development of each Germanic dialect. Thus, in the dative singular masculine-neuter, the extension took place in all of the dialects: Got. *blindamma*, 'to the blind,' OHG. *blintemu*, OS. *blindum*—and OI. *spǫkom*, 'to the sensible.' However, in the dative singular feminine, Gothic kept the form of the substantive type, *blindai*, while OHG. has *blinteru* and OS. has *blinderu*. Old Icelandic normally has the demonstrative form *spakre*, 'to the sensible,' but Old Swedish still has forms such as *halve*, 'to the half,' which is of the substantive type. The extension, then, took place little by little, and we can still follow its progress in part during the historical period.

The recent character of the influence of the demonstratives results from the fact that the nasal of the accusative singular masculine, preserved only by the monosyllabic character of forms like OHG. *den*, appears in the adjective: OHG. *blinten* and, with the particle -*a* appended, Got. *blindana*.

In the nominative-accusative singular neuter, the Indo-European adjectives signifying "one," "all," "same" did not have the ending *-*t*(-*d*) of the demonstratives; Sanskrit has *ékam*, 'one,' *sárvam*, 'all,' and so forth. This is how we explain why the substantive form of the type Got. *juk* was maintained in the nominative-accusative neuter Got. *blind* as well as in Old High German *blint*, Old Saxon *blind*, and so on. Secondarily the demonstrative form was introduced: Gothic has *blindata* beside *blind*, and Old High German has *blintaz* beside *blint*. Nordic tended to generalize the -*t* of the demonstratives, but traces of forms such as *all*, 'all,' are still numerous.

Thus Germanic has characterized the adjective by means of the inflection of the "demonstrative" type.

However, this inflection is heavy, and a phrase like Got. *þamma blindamma*, 'to this blind (man),' would seem to be somewhat unpleasant. Germanic remedied this inconvenience by taking recourse to the inflection of stems in -*n*-, which it developed widely. An adjective like Got. masculine *blinds*, neuter *blind*, and feminine *blinda* is then supplemented by a form with an -*n*- type suffix called weak: Got. masc. *blinda*, neuter *blindo* (gen. sg. masc.-neuter *blindins*), and fem. *blindo* (gen. sg. *blindons*). This inflection of the adjective agrees with that for substantives with stems in -*n*-. It is the one which is always used when the adjective is accompanied by a demonstrative. It continues an Indo-European type which is represented in several other languages, notably Greek and Latin, but in these languages the type in -*n*- furnishes derived substantives; thus, in Greek, *ouraniōn*, 'inhabitant of the sky,' is derived from *ouránios*, 'celestial.' Therefore, an expression such as OI. *Haraldr unge* signifies etymologically 'Harold the young man.'

The adjectives which were from ancient stems in -*n*- naturally have only this inflection called weak. The demonstrative inflection could extend only to adjectives with stems in -*a*- for the masculine-neuter and in -*ō*- for the feminine. The Gothic comparative in -*iza* (for example, *managiza*, 'more numerous,' beside *manags*, 'numerous'), which corresponds to the Greek type in -*iōn*, gen. -*ionos* (ancient *-*is-ōn*, *-*is-on-os*), does not have inflections of the "demonstrative" type. There are a good many adjectives like Got. *fruma*, 'the first,' *sama*, 'the same,' and so forth which are always in -*n*-.

However, most adjectives show the inflection of the demonstratives, some because from an ancient date they have belonged to the thematic type of Lat. *nouos*, others because they have been adapted to it.

Common Germanic inherited an important number of adjective stems in -*u*-, such as Got. *kaurus*, 'heavy,' which corresponds to Skr. *gurúḥ*, 'heavy,' and Gr. *barús*. We know from Greek that certain of these adjectives used a combination of the suffixes *-*eu*- and *-*yo*-; for example, the Greek has *polús*, 'abundant,' in the nominative masculine singular and *polú* in the nominative-accusative singular neuter. Germanic corresponds with Got. *filu*, 'much,' with the root vocalism in *e*, which is also found in OIr. *il* (ancient *pelu). But we find beside the forms above the Gr. gen. *polloû*, nom. pl. *polloí*, and so on, from a stem in *-*yo*-, *polyo-. In Germanic the adjective stems in -*u*- keep the -*u*- only in the nominative singular; the rest of the declension is in -*ja*- in the masculine-neuter and in -*jō*- in the feminine. Thus, in the accusative singular we find Got. *hardjana* for the masculine and *hardja* for the feminine, opposite the nominative singular *hardus*, 'hard' (masculine and feminine). In the other languages, the *u* is no longer visible in the nominative, and in West Germanic the nominative itself has changed to the type in *-ja-*. Therefore, opposite Skr. *tr̥ṣúḥ*, 'desirous' (literally, 'dried from desire, thirsty from'), and Got. *þaursus*, 'dry,' we have OE. *þyrre*, OS. *thurri*, and OHG. *durri*; Old Icelandic has *þurr* without inflection, but Old Swedish has *þørr*, with an inflection which reveals the *-ja*. Thus, with the adjectives in *-u-* having almost all their forms in *-ja-*, the weak inflection appears in these forms normally; opposite Got. *hardus*, 'hard,' acc. masc. *hardjana*, we have the weak form nom. masc. sg. *hardja*, acc. masc. sg. *hardjana*, and so forth.

The Germanic adjective is characterized not only by the ancient fact that it distinguishes three genders in accordance with the substantive which it modifies, but also by the new fact that it has, as a general rule, two inflections, one demonstrative, the other in *-n-*.

German has kept down to the present the double inflection of the adjective which began to be manifest in common Germanic. In addition, thanks to the loss of the final sibilant in the nominative masculine singular and to the conservation of the old nominal type in the nominative neuter, German constituted an invariable form for the predicate—for example, *blind*—so that modern German has two inflections for the adjective directly modifying a substantive as well as an invariable form for the predicate.

On the other hand, languages like English, which early eliminated the finals, have tended to constitute an invariable adjective in all cases and to eliminate the special characteristics that common Germanic had given to the adjective. From this action, the notion of grammatical gender, the expression of which was one of the most original features of Indo-European, lost its principal support. In English it has disappeared, and the only trace of it left is in the pronouns for the third-person singular.

Chapter XI

Accessory Words and Word Order

THE PROGRESSIVE reduction of inflection has had the same effects in Germanic that it has had everywhere else. It has brought about the use of word order as a means of grammatical expression, as well as the use of accessory words.

In common Germanic, where the inflection was still rich and varied, the order of words was flexible and had no grammatical value. No grammatical function was indicated by the position of the word. In translating the Bible, Ulfila was able to keep almost entirely the order of the words in Greek, which had no grammatical meaning.

However, word order soon tended to become fixed, and, as it became fixed, it acquired grammatical values. For example, in Gothic, interrogation is marked by particles: "do you wish?" in Gothic is *wileiz-u*; the particle *u* placed after *wileis* (ancient *wileiz* with -*z* preserved before a vowel) expresses interrogation. In the Western dialects and in Nordic, interrogation is marked by the order of words: the subject is placed regularly after the verb in interrogative sentences, as we see, for example, in Old High German *wil thū*, 'do you wish?'

Word order is fixed even in German, where inflection still exists, although it has been reduced, and where many forms are ambiguous. In English it is one of the principal modes of expressing grammatical categories, and, as in French, it is only the position of a noun in relation to the verb which indicates in an English sentence whether that noun is subject or object of the verb. The complicated inflection of Indo-European was eliminated without inconvenience: it has been replaced by a method which is both elegant and simple.

However, the order of words is not sufficient to express their relationships. There are many varied relationships which must be expressed by accessory words. The prepositions which serve this purpose have been grouped with nouns and have tended to express what Indo-European rendered by the locative, the ablative—this was already accomplished in common Germanic—and, finally, even the genitive or the dative. This is the stage which English has reached, while German still has a genitive and a dative whose characteristics have been renewed but whose role scarcely differs from that of the Indo-European case forms of the same name.

In Indo-European, prepositions were autonomous words which were not united to either nouns or verbs. In a Homeric sentence like *ek d'ágage klisíēs Brisēída,* 'he led Briséis from the tent,' *ek,* 'out of,' is linked neither to the verb *ágage,* 'he led,' nor to *klisíēs,* 'from the tent'; it is a word, originally autonomous, which indicates the point of departure and applies to the entire sentence. In Indo-European, these words are called preverbal prepositions. With time, these little words were grouped either with the noun, as in *ek klisíēs,* 'out of the tent,' or with the verb, as in *ekságage,* 'he led out' (with the form *eks* for the preposition before a vowel). This state of things had already been reached in common Germanic: there were, on the one hand, prepositions with nouns and, on the other, preverbs with verbs.

The development of the prepositions was completed only in the course of the particular history of each of the various Germanic dialects; certain prepositions, like Got., OHG., and OE. *in* and OI. *i,* opposite Gr. *eni, en* and Lat. *in,* 'in,' are common Germanic, but many others differ from dialect to dialect.

Germanic preverbs form one entity with the verb to which they are joined, and the fusion has reached the point where certain preverbs serve only to indicate the degree of completion of the action. Such is often the role of the preverb *ga-* in Gothic; *fullnan* signifies 'to fill up' (progressively), while *gafullnan* signifies 'to be filled up.' For example, in Luke II, 40, it is said that 'the child grew, becoming full of wisdom'; the Gothic translator writes *fullnands handugeins.* But, in Luke I, 41, it is said that Elisabeth "was filled with the Holy Spirit"; here the Gothic translator writes *gafullnoda ahmins weihis,* and in this instance *ga-,* 'with,' no longer has any concrete value. Nevertheless, in Gothic *ga-* still has a trace of autonomy in that particles can be inserted between *ga-* and the following verb, as is the case with the particle *u* in *ga-u-laubeis,* 'do you believe?'

The use of *ga-* to indicate the completion of the action is free and general in Gothic. In Old High German it tends to be fixed to the passive past participle, and we find *gi-buntan,* 'bound,' opposite *bintu,* 'I bind,' and *bant,* 'I have bound.' A free use of *gi-* to indicate that the verb expresses a completed action still exists in Old High German and disappeared only later, whereas the use of *gi-* become *ge-* has persisted in the past participle. Thus a preverb, which was an autonomous word in Indo-European and still to some degree autonomous in common Germanic, tends to be only an accessory element of a grammatical form in German.

Accessory words became fused with principal words and served either to mark a form more clearly, as when in Old High German *bintis*, 'you bind,' is replaced by *bintist(u)*, with a pronoun appended, or to form new categories: the reflexive *sik* furnishes in Nordic a sort of reflexive and passive, for example OI. *kallask*, 'to be called, to call oneself,' opposite *kalla*, 'to call.'

Indo-European, in which each word was autonomous, did not have an article. Common Germanic did not have one either, and Gothic still did not have one in the fourth century A.D. However, certain demonstratives before nouns assumed a value that was increasingly accessory; in West Germanic it is the demonstrative OE. (acc.) *done*, OS. (nom.) *thē*, and OHG. *der*, placed before the noun, and in Nordic it is the demonstrative *-enn*, placed after the noun and forming one body with it. Thus the role of an accessory word such as the article increased little by little, until the article became an essential element of the language. Comparable developments took place in other languages, in Greek from an early date, in Romance, in Celtic, and in Armenian, while other Indo-European languages, notably the Slavic languages in which the case inflection has persisted, still do not have an article today.

The tendency to replace inflection by word order and accessory words is universal in Indo-European. Nowhere is it more strongly manifested than in the Germanic languages, although Germanic still maintains an archaic aspect. Nowhere has it been carried out more completely than in English. English represents the extreme limit of a development: it exhibits a type different from the common Indo-European type and has kept almost nothing of Indo-European morphology.

PART THREE

VOCABULARY

Chapter XII

Retained Indo-European Elements

ON THE one hand the Indo-European vocabulary contained isolated words designating a specific concept, such as the nouns for "daughter-in-law" (Gr. *nyós*, Arm. *nu*, and so on), "sheep" (Skr. *ávih*, Lat. *ouis*, and so on), and "liver" (Skr. *yákṛt*, Gr. *hêpar*, Lat. *iecur*, and so on). On the other hand, it contained "roots" to which verbal or nominal forms were attached; for example, in Greek, from the Indo-European root **dō-*, **dǝ-*, 'to give' (Gr. *dō-*, *do-*), we have *dí-dō-mi*, 'I give,' *é-dō-ka*, 'I have given,' *é-do-men*, 'we have given,' *dǒ-tōr*, 'donor,' *dó-sis*, 'action of giving,' *dǒ-s*, 'gift,' and *dǒ-ron*, 'gift.' Each of the words attached to a root is independent of the others, and none of those which have just been cited is derived from one of the others or ordered by one of the others. However, these words can supply derivatives; for example, from Gr. *dǒ-ron*, 'gift,' we have *dōréō*, 'I make a gift,' and from *dōréō* we have *dórēma*, 'act of making a gift.' A family of Indo-European words can thus ramify in various ways.

Germanic has preserved Indo-European isolated nouns. For example, Got. *dauhtar*, 'daughter,' corresponds to Gr. *thygátēr* and Lit. *duktē* (acc. *dùkterį*); Got. *daur*, 'door,' represents the Indo-European word found in Arm. *durk*, 'door,' Gr. *thyrai*, Lat. *forēs*, and so forth. This is the case with a number of isolated words. Got. *þiuda*, 'people' (OI. *þiod*, OE. *þeod*, and OHG. *diota*) corresponds to Lettish *tauta*, OI. *tūath*, and Oscan *touto*, 'people'; it is one of those words that belongs to a group of dialects extending from Italo-Celtic to Celtic and Slavic, and passing through Germanic. These words reveal the civilization of Western and Northern Europe. The number of isolated words of this sort is not great, but they are in current use and hold an important place in the Germanic language.

Often the words preserved take on a new aspect by the addition of secondary suffixes; thus we have seen (on p. 90) how Got. *atta*, *qino*, and *hairto* became stems in *-n-*. Under the influence of the accusative in *-u(n)*, Got. *fotu*, the noun for 'foot,' became a stem in *-u-*: Got. *fotus* (nominative) (see p. 64).

As for the roots, they ceased furnishing nominal forms parallel to the strong verbs. They became verbal, whereas in Indo-European they furnished both nouns and verbs.

The ancient suffix for agent nouns, *-ter-*, which supplied Greek with the types *dōtōr* and *dotḗr*, 'donor,' and Latin with the type *dator*, is no longer represented in Germanic.

The suffix *-tei-*, which formed abstract nouns and which, in the form -si-, remained productive in Greek for example, persists in Germanic in numerous cases. It was still distinct in common Germanic, so the link with verbal forms continued to be felt. In Gothic especially, the preverb which served to indicate that the verb itself expressed a completed action figured among the representatives of this formation. However, phonetic circumstances gave various aspects to the suffix; it lost all unity, and, as a consequence, it ceased to be productive from the beginning of the historical period. In addition, the loss of -i- in final syllables reduced it to a consonant in the nominative and the accusative. From the root IE. *men-*, 'to think' (represented by Got. *man*, 'he thinks,' and so on), we get IE. *mṇ-tei*, 'thought' (Skr. *matíḥ*, 'thought,' Lat. *mens*, from *mentis*, and so forth), Got. *ga-munds*, 'memory,' OE. *ge-mynd*, and OHG. *gi-munt*. After *s, f,* and *x* we have -t-. Thus, opposite Got. *giban*, 'to give' (*fra-giban*, 'to give back'), we have Got. *fra-gifts*, 'putting back, delivery,' and OHG. *gift*, 'gift'; opposite Got. *siuks*, 'ill,' and OHG. *sioh*, we have OHG. *suht*, 'illness'; opposite Got. *mag*, 'he can,' we have *mahts*, 'power'; and opposite Got. *lais*, 'he knows,' and *laisjan*, 'to teach' (OHG. *lēran*), we have *lists*, 'cleverness, ruse.' Although broadly represented and productive to the time of common Germanic, the ancient formation in *-tei-* has changed character, and the words in which it is included have become isolated little by little. We no longer feel in modern German the relation between the substantive *zucht* and the verb *ziehen* for example.

Moreover, many nouns which were attached directly to a root appear isolated in Germanic because the verbal forms of the root have gone out of use. Let us take the neuter noun Got. *liuhaþ*, 'light' (OE. *lēoht* and OHG. *lioht*); this is an ancient *leukoto-*, from a root *leuk-*, which is represented by Lat. *lūceō*, 'I shine,' and by Skr. *rócate*, 'he shines.' Like most Indo-European languages, Germanic has not kept any verbal forms of this root.

Some words, originally of the same root, have become separated because their meanings have diverged. We no longer see how Got. *liufs*, 'dear,' OI. *liūfr*, and OHG. *liob* (cf. OSl. *ljubŭ*, 'dear') are related to OI. *lof*, 'praise,' and OHG. *lob* (OI. *lofa*, 'to praise,' and OHG. *lobōn*), or to Got. *ga-laubjan*, 'to believe,' and OHG. *gi-louben*, or to Got. *lubains*, 'hope,' all of which are representatives of the root IE. *leubh-*, 'to love,' but which in Germanic form as many distinct groups.

In short, Germanic words appear isolated and are no longer grouped around roots. There are words derived from other words, such as OHG. *lobōn*, 'to praise,' from *lob*, 'praise'; but there are no longer large families of words which include both nouns and verbs freely grouped around a single root, as was characteristic of the Indo-European type.

Although a good many vestiges of the ancient Indo-European formations remain, the Germanic vocabulary has acquired an aspect different from that of Indo-European. This is because the types of these formations have ceased to produce new words and have even ceased to be understood.

Chapter XIII

Transformed Indo-European Elements

WORDS AND types of formations preserved from Indo-European could not suffice for the development of the Germanic language.

As we have just seen, the general change of linguistic type and the phonetic and semantic alterations increasingly obscured the processes of formation of Indo-European words, and this led to the replacement of these processes by new ones.

Suffixes whose forms had been excessively reduced were replaced by longer ones. The following example provides a good illustration of the method.

There was in Indo-European a suffix *-teu- which furnished nouns indicating an act. For instance, from a root *geus-, 'to taste,' we have in Latin gus-tu-s, 'act of tasting'; the corresponding Gothic word is kustus, 'test, examination' (beside the verbs -kiusan, 'to experience,' and kausjan, 'to taste, examine'). Representatives such as this of the suffix *-teu- are not lacking in Germanic. However, in its simple form, this suffix ceased to furnish new words. Moreover, Germanic developed a type of derived verb in *-atjan such as Got. lauh-atjan, 'to shine,' and OHG. lohazzan and laugazzan, 'to flame,' from the root *leuk-, which figures in Got. liuhaþ, 'light' (see above, p. 106). By adding the suffix *-tu- to *-at- of these verbs, we obtain *-assu-, since -t plus t- becomes -ss- in Germanic. If then from *ebnaz, 'equal,' we derive the verb *ebnatjan, 'to equalize' (attested by OE. emnettan), we obtain from it a substantive, Got. ibnassus, 'equality,' and OE. emness. This substantive is the abstract noun corresponding to the adjective *ebnaz. Following this model, we obtain from a verb such as horinon, 'to commit adultery,' an abstract noun, horinassus, 'adultery,' and we are able to extract from words of this kind a suffix, Got. -inassus, which is distinctive, quite long, and destined to become productive. For example, from Got. blotan, 'to honor,' we can derive bloti-nassus, 'cult'; likewise, in Old English, from ehtan, 'to pursue,' we get ehtness, 'persecution,' from gōd, 'good,' we get gōdness, 'goodness,' and so forth. This suffix has endured down to the present in English, where, for example, we still find the word goodness.

The relatively clear and long suffixes which Germanic obtained by processes of the sort just briefly described were not the only ones the language obtained. Another process furnished some that were still more distinct. From Indo-European, Germanic inherited the habit of joining two nouns to form one noun, a procedure which we call "composition." Consider, for example, a word like Got. *haidus*, 'sort, manner,' OI. *heidr*, 'dignity,' OE. *hād*, and OHG. *heit*, 'condition, rank,' a word which corresponds to Skr. *ketúḥ*, 'sign'; it serves as the second member of West Germanic compounds such as OHG. *magat-heit*, 'state of being a maiden, virginity,' and OE. *māeden-hād*, 'maidenhood.' As there were several compounds using this noun as a second member, and as the word OE. *hād* and OHG. *heit* had an abstract meaning, it lost its original value as a noun, and in English *maiden-hood*, *-hood* behaves like a suffix; the corresponding *-heit* has become a very productive suffix in German. This process played an important role in the development of Germanic languages and furnished several important suffixes, such as *-tum* in German.

Procedures of derivation were not the only ones to be renewed. Many ideas received new designations, often without any obvious reason for the change.

For example, words for certain parts of the body were transformed or replaced because the ancient term was the object of some prohibition. The belief in the evil eye had as its consequence the replacement or a change in form of the ancient noun for "eye" in several Indo-European languages. The Germanic term, Got. *augo*, OI. *auga*, OE. *ēage*, and OHG. *ouga*, recalls the ancient noun, of which Lit. *akis* and OSl. *oko* give a good idea. In this case, there was undoubtedly some artificial arrangement, possibly influenced by the word for "ear" as in Got. *auso*, OI. *eyra*, OE. *ēare*, and OHG. *ōra* (with *ō* representing *au* before *r*; in Nordic and in West Germanic we have the representatives of *z* opposite Gothic *s*); cf. Lit. *ausis* and OSl. *uxo*. The form corresponding to Lat. *caput*, 'head,' was preserved in OI. *hǫfod* and OE. *hafud*; but the word for "head" varies from one Indo-European language to another, and the old name was deformed in Germanic by contamination with the group OI. *hūfa*, OE. *hūfe*, and OHG. *hūba*. 'cap.' Thus, we have Got. *haubiþ*, OI. *haufud*, OE. *hēafod*, and OHG. *haubit*. The words for "hand" are also diverse in the Indo-European languages: Skr. *hástah*, Gr. *kheír*, Lat. *manus*, and Lit. *rankà*, for example. Germanic has a special word: Got. *handus*, OI. *hǫnd*, OE. *hond*, and OHG. *hant*, which is doubtlessly related to Got. *-hinþan*, 'to take possession of,' just as Lit. *rankà* is related to *renkù*, 'to pick up.'

Forms of anomalous type tend to be eliminated if they are not in very frequent use. The verb forms from the root IE. *$p\bar{o}(i)$-, *pi-, 'to drink' (Gr. *pí-nō*, 'I drink,' Lat. *pō-culum*, 'drinking vessel,' and so on), were very strange, as we can see in Skr. *píbati*, 'he drinks,' OIr. *ibid*, and Lat. *bibit*. They either disappeared or were normalized in most languages. Here Germanic has a special word, which looks very Indo-European but has no counterpart in any other language of the family: Got. *drigkan*, 'to drink,' OI. *drekka*, OE. *drincan*, and OHG. *trinkan*.

Some short words were enlarged by adding secondary suffixes. Thus, the ancient word for "dog," which was clearly preserved in Skr. *ç(u)vá* (gen. *çúnah*), Gr. *kýōn* (gen. *kynós*), OIr. *cū* (gen. *con*), and Lit. *šŭ* (gen. *šuñs*), was represented in Germanic by *hun-da-*: Got. *hunds*, OI. *hundr*, OE. *hund*, and OHG. *hunt*.

Certain groups of words acquired special meanings and were limited to conveying only a small part of their former meanings. For example, the root IE. *$leik^w$-, 'to leave, to remain,' of Skr. *riṇdkti*, 'he leaves,' Lat. *linquit*, Gr. *leípō*, 'I leave,' and Lit. *lëkù*, was maintained in Got. *leihwan*, OI. *liá*, OE. *-léon*, and OHG. *lihan*, which mean simply 'to lend'; already in Indo-European the root was used to designate transmissions of objects having value, and the substantives OI. *lán*, 'loan,' OE. *láen*, and OHG. *léhan* should be compared with Skr. *réknah*, 'heritage'; Germanic kept only this technical meaning. A part of the meaning of *$leik^w$-, that of 'to leave,' was expressed by an ancient root, *$l\bar{e}d$-, from which we get Got. *letan*, OI. *láta*, OE. *láetan*, and OHG. *lázan*, as well as Got. *lats*, 'cowardly, soft,' OI. *latr*, OE. *laet*, and OHG. *laz* (cf. Lat. *lassus* and so forth). Another part of the meaning, that of 'to remain,' was expressed by the root *leip-, 'to stick, to remain stuck to' (cf. OSl. *lipēti*, 'to be adherent to,' and Gr. *lípos*, 'grease') in Gothic *bi-liban*, 'to remain,' OE. *be-lifa*, OHG. *bi-liban*, and Got. *af-lifnan*. From this root *leip-, a verb expressing condition has taken on a special meaning: Got. *liban*, 'to live,' OI. *lifa*, and OHG. *lebēn*. This verb replaced the Indo-European verb represented by Skr. *jívati*, 'he lives,' OSl. *živetŭ*, and Lat. *uiuit*, a verb which had anomalous forms and showed different aspects in different languages.

By various actions, the details of which would be endless, Germanic transformed most of the Indo-European elements of its vocabulary. It modified both forms and meanings and most often created something new. If by chance we lacked all traditional information about the Germanic vocabulary, we would find it embarrassing to try to explain Germanic texts with only the aid of an etymologic dictionary of the ancient Indo-European languages.

The way in which the Indo-European vocabulary—the vocabulary of an aristocracy concerned with politics, law, and religion—was adapted or replaced in the Germanic languages is illustrated by the history of the word for "woman." Indo-European had a word inflected in an irregular manner. Germanic kept two of its forms, which were normalized and differentiated by their meanings. Alternating forms with roots $*g^wen$- and $*g^{wo}n$- (Ir. *ben* and Gr. *gynē*) furnished derivatives in -*n*-: on the one hand, we have Got. *qino* (from which we get *qinakunds* and *qineins*, 'feminine'), OS. *quena*, and so forth; on the other hand, we have OI. *kona*, which designate a person of the female sex. From a form with vowel *ē*, which corresponds to Vedic -*jāni*-, a stem in -*i*- was derived: Got. *gens*, designating a 'married woman, matron.' Continuing to evolve, the words for a "female person" acquired the meaning "prostitute" in English *quean* and Swedish *kona*; conversely, the word for "matron" became English *queen*. To designate a person of female sex, Germanic introduced a neuter substantive of unknown origin: OI. *vif*, OE. *wif*, and OHG. *wib*. In turn, English differentiated *wife*, 'married woman,' and *woman* (from *wif-man*).

Chapter XIV

Ancient Borrowings

BETWEEN THE time when Germanic became isolated from the other Indo-European dialects and the time when the most ancient texts were fixed in written form, Germanic adopted a great number of foreign words.

Some of these words are found in other Indo-European languages, but we are unable to say from what idioms, doubtlessly non-Indo-European, the borrowings were made.

For example, the word for "silver" is *sĭrebro* in Slavic, *siraplis*, *sirablan* in Old Prussian, *sidābras* in Lithuanian, and *sudrabs* in Lettish, and the corresponding Germanic forms are Got. *silubr*, OI. *silfr*, OE. *seolfor*, and OHG. *silbar*. The divergences among these various words indicate that it is a question of borrowings made independently from some unknown language.

The Gothic word *paida*, OE. *pād*, OHG. *pfeit*, which designates a type of garment, can be compared with Gr. *baítē*, a garment worn by a shepherd, which seems to be in Greek a word of foreign origin.

The word for "hemp," OI. *hanpr*, OE. *haenep*, and OHG. *hanaf*, is obviously to be compared with Gr. *kánnabis*, which designates the same plant. This word is not Indo-European; its very form proclaims it to be a foreign word.

The number of cases of this sort is restricted. The other borrowings, which we can recognize, have been made by Germanic from neighboring Indo-European languages, at times and under circumstances we can at least surmise.

When, from the fifth to the third century B.C., the Gauls founded their empire of such short duration, they developed a brilliant civilization which exercised an influence on their neighbors. Undoubtedly the borrowings of Germanic from Gallic date back to this period.

It is known that the metallurgy of iron was well developed by the Gauls. It is not then surprising that the Germanic word for "iron," Got. *eisarn*, OI. *isarn*, OE. *isern*, and OHG. *isarn*, is of Celtic origin; the Celtic form is Gallic *isarno-*, preserved in *Isarno-Dori*, 'Gates of Iron,' Ir. *iarn*, and Welsh *haiarn*.

The Indo-European word for "king" is preserved only in Sanskrit and Italo-Celtic: Skr. *rā́j-*, Lat. *rēx* (*rēgis*), and OIr. *ri* (gen. *rig*). It had an *ē* which Celtic changed to *i*: Gallic *rig-* (*Dumnorig-* and so forth). Germanic borrowed the word with the Celtic *i* before the consonant mutation: Got. *reiks*, 'chief,' OI. *rikr*, and the derived OE. *rice*, OS. *riki*, and OHG. *rihhi* (with the same meaning). The Germanic words which mean "king" are secondary derivatives formed from Germanic elements: Got. *þiudans*, 'king,' is derived from *þiuda*, 'nation,' just as Lat. *dominus*, 'head of the house, master,' is derived from *domus*, 'house'; and OI. *konungr*, 'king,' OE. *cyning*, OS. *cuning*, and OHG. *kuning* are derived from the word for "tribe," Got. *kuni*, and so on.

The Gallic word *ambactos*, 'servant,' was also borrowed: OE. *ambeht* and OHG. *ambaht*; Old Icelandic has only the feminine *ambátt*; Gothic germanized the word by a popular etymology using the preverb *and-*, whence *andbahts*. The word has enjoyed extensive development in German since the derived OHG. *ambahti*, 'service,' has become the well-known term *Amt*.

There is no doubt that numerous terms of civilization common to Germanic and to Celtic are borrowings in Germanic. Thus the word for "doctor," Got. *lekeis*, OE. *lǣce*, and OHG. *lāhhi*, is a borrowing from Gallic **lēgyo-* (in which *ē* represents an ancient diphthong); Irish has kept *liaig*, 'doctor.'

The Roman Empire, which extended to the Rhine and the Danube, was in contact with Germanic-speaking populations along a long frontier. During the whole imperial epoch, Roman merchants traded with Germans, and Germans served in the Roman legions. The influence of Roman civilization on Germany was very great. Then came Christianity, which was spread especially by missionaries for whom Latin was the scholarly language. Thus many Latin words passed into Germanic.

Germanic unity no longer existed at the dates when these borrowings took place; but the Germanic languages were still very much alike, and, passing from one dialect to another, the words were adapted because the speakers had the feeling of the transpositions to be made in order to adapt the forms to each dialect. The recent date of these borrowings is marked by the fact that, unlike the borrowings from Celtic, they are posterior to the consonant mutation of common Germanic (and anterior to the special mutations of Old High German). However, they were entirely germanized and received the initial accent of intensity. Some examples will give an idea of the procedures used.

Latin *catinus*, 'dish,' had a derivative, *catillus*; from it came the Germanic word preserved in Got. *katile* (gen. plural), OI. *ketell*, OE. *cytel*, and OHG. *kezzil*, 'cauldron.'

The donkey is a Mediterranean animal; it was not known in the ancient Indo-European world. The Germans borrowed the name for this animal from the Latin *asellus*: Got. *asilus*, OE. *esol, eosol,* and OHG. *esil.*

The Latin word *arca,* 'chest, small box,' provided Got. *arka,* OI. *ork,* OE. *earc,* and OHG. *archa.*

The most striking testimony of the importance of Latin influence appears in a suffix for agent nouns. The Latin suffix *-ārius* furnished the Romance languages with their suffix for agent nouns; it appears in Italian in the form *-ajo,* in French in the form *-ier.* Now, the Germanic languages acquired enough of these Latin words, such as *scolārius,* 'school-boy, scholar,' beside *scola,* 'school' (OHG. *scuolāri,* beside *scuola*), that the suffix became productive over the entire domain. On the model of Lat. *liber: librārius,* Gothic has *bokāreis,* 'scribe,' from *boka,* 'letter,' and *bokos,* 'book'; it has likewise *laisāreis,* 'teacher,' from *laisjan,* 'to teach,' just as Old High German has *lērāri,* from *lēran.* Infrequent in Gothic, this suffix is commonly used in the domain where Roman influence was most directly felt: in the West Germanic domain. The borrowing of Latin *-ārius* took place at a relatively late period, at a time when Germanic no longer transformed *ā* into *ō,* and when it had again acquired an *ā*: the correspondence of Got. *a* (that is, *ā*) with OHG. *ā,* in an unstressed syllable, is sufficient to indicate the recent character of the borrowing of *-ārius.*

The influence of the Church of Rome is manifested sometimes by the borrowing of manners of expression: the compound Got. *arma-hairts,* OHG. *arm-herz,* 'merciful,' is an evident transfer of the Latin compound *miseri-cors* and attests in its way to the intensity of the Roman influence. However, this transfer shows that an effort was made to find Germanic equivalents for Christian terms. For example, for "to fast," the term used was Got. *fastan,* OI. *fasta,* and OE. *faestan,* that is, literally 'to hold fast' an observance; it is an old pagan term, preserved with a Christian adaptation.

There were also missionaries from the Eastern Church, but their influence on vocabulary appears only in West Germanic where we find several Christian words taken from Greek: OE. *cirice,* OS. *kirika,* and OHG. *kiricha,* 'church,' are forms derived from the Greek word *kyriakḗ.* In Gothic, *aikklesjo* is a learned transcription of the Greek *ekklēsíā* from the written language.

All of these foreign influences gave to the ancient Germanic languages a good number of cultural terms. On the whole, however, the vocabulary of these languages is composed of Indo-European elements preserved or transformed. It is only in the more advanced periods of their development that certain languages became filled with foreign elements. English in particular, under the influence of the Norman nobility, the church, and medieval science, became a language full of Latin and French elements, so that the vocabulary of modern English is half Latin and Romance.

Without undergoing such an extensive Latin and Romance influence, all of the other Germanic languages received many Latin words. Old High German even took the Latin *scribere*, 'to write,' from which it formed the strong verb *skriban* (there were no common Germanic words meaning "to read" and "to write"). The number of Latin and Romance words increased until the end of the nineteenth century.

The influence of Latin, the common learned language of the Middle Ages throughout the West, had another noteworthy aspect: the words of the Germanic languages acquired the values of corresponding Latin words, while other words were modeled on Latin words. Thus, OHG. *gi-wizzani*, 'conscience' (modern Ger. *Gewissen*), was modeled on Lat. *con-scientia*. Even where it consists of native linguistic elements, the vocabulary of Germanic languages is filled with the action of Latin. In spite of appearances, there is thus a great difference between the common Germanic vocabulary and the vocabularies of the modern Germanic languages.

The very Germanic appearance of modern German is deceptive. The uses of words are largely transpositions of the uses of medieval Latin words or of their corresponding modern French equivalents. Many formations are simple transfers. With Germanic elements, words like *Eindruck* and *Ausdruck* are nothing more than Fr. *impression* and *expression*, which themselves are the Latin words *impressiō* and *expressiō* slightly adapted. German words are thus, in a large measure, Latin or Romance words provided with a Germanic mask. Like France, Germany took part in the Carolingian renaissance; with all of Western Europe, it had Latin as its learned language until well along in the modern period. The ruin of the Roman Empire brought about a great cultural decline and, at the same time, a refreshening owing to contact with what remained of the particular civilizations of Central and Northern Europe. Nevertheless, the civilization of Western Europe continued that of the Roman Empire. As a language of civilization, German is then largely a Latin language transposed to the linguistic system of Germanic. The Scandinavian languages at first resisted this trend because the Scandinavian world had preserved old Germanic traditions and usages; but, in the course of the Middle Ages, they yielded in their turn.

Chapter XV

Word Composition

INDO-EUROPEAN used, to a considerable extent, groups of two stems, the first without inflection, the second inflected, which were brought together to form nouns. Latin thus had compounds such as *in-iustus, bi-pes, agri-cola,* and so forth. These compounds had definite forms which characterized them; thus in Latin *ex-torris,* opposite *terra,* we observe both a suffix which indicates the adjective and a vocalic alternation—*o* opposite the *e* of the simple form.

This process was used especially in the learned language. Germanic, on the other hand, which by the beginning of the historical period hardly reflected any longer the ancient Indo-European civilization, kept very little of it. The type called "possessive," such as Lat. *in-ops,* 'one who has no resources,' *quadru-pes,* 'one which has four feet,' and *prae-ceps,* 'one who has his head forward,' is scarcely represented. The type with a verb as the first member like Gr. *phygo-ptólemos,* 'one who flees war,' is not found at all.

Moreover, intervening changes in the structure of the language obscured the original stems. Thus, in accordance with a general rule of Indo-European, the final element of the first member of a compound lost its vowel. Therefore, parallel to the negation **ne,* which is clearly preserved in Got. *ni* and Ger. *ni-wiht* (literally, 'not a thing,' whence modern Ger. *nicht*), the form of the first member of the compound was **n̥-,* which resulted in Gr. *a-* and Germanic *un-.* From the Germanic point of view, *un-* no longer has any perceptible relation to *ni.* The result is that if Gothic has on the one hand *ni kann,* 'he does not know,' and on the other *un-kunþs,* 'unknown,' the two types no longer have anything in common. In the Germanic languages *un-* is no longer a word forming the first member of a compound; it is a prefix which transforms a positive meaning to a negative meaning and is used to oppose Ger. *un-richtig* to *richtig* and so forth.

An ancient form used as the first member of a compound, such as Ger. *ga-,* which is equivalent in meaning to Lat. *cum,* can persist only in compounds, and, from then on, it loses all individuality. In a word like

Ger. *Gebirge, ge-* is a prefix which indicates a whole, opposite *Berg*; it is no longer a question of composition. In a word like Ger. *gleich* or English *alike*, we no longer detect the ancient compound **ga-lika-* 'the body of which is similar.'

Word composition of the Indo-European type ceased to play a role in Germanic: insofar as vestiges of it subsist, true compounds are no longer recognized in them.

The compounds which are found in great numbers in the Germanic languages from a historical date, notably in German, are of a new type and result from the new structure of the language. While the Indo-European sentence was composed of autonomous words freely arranged, the Germanic sentence since the Middle Ages has been composed of groups of words arranged in a fixed order. The group unity in English is marked in a striking manner by the fact that with a group such as *all good old men* the *'s* of the possessive applies to the whole phrase: *all good old men's works*. In German, *die junge Frau* forms a bound group, no element of which can be shifted. Moreover, the degree of autonomy of the words in the Germanic sentence is marked by the relative intensity of the accent: the elements subordinated to others are accentuated with less force. Words grouped in a fixed manner and accentuated with a different intensity lend themselves to the expression of a single notion: in the German phrase *eine junge Frau*, there are two distinct notions. By bringing together *jung* and *Frau*, as the language tends naturally to do by virtue of its phonetic and morphologic structure, we obtain a word OHG. *iunkfrouua* (in which the accentuation on *frouua* is attested), modern Ger. *Jungfrau*, which has the value of Lat. *puella*. French has followed the same procedure: although written as two words, *jeune fille* is one word, expressing a single idea, and this is so true that in familiar speech we can say, "*c'est trop jeune fille.*" If the two elements *jung-* and *-frau* keep accents, the one primary, the other secondary, the word remains a compound. Only partially united, the two terms can be felt separately by the speaker; such is the case with Ger. *Jungfrau*. If, on the contrary, the word is unified completely and if it is submitted to the general rule of the language, which, in this case, accentuates the initial syllable and sacrifices the rest, the result will be a form like Ger. *Jungfer*, in which the first element remains clear and the second is obscured. In this particular case, German possesses both words, *Jungfrau* and *Jungfer*.

The composition thus obtained furnished the Germanic languages with a flexible and convenient procedure for the formation of nouns. When the compound is treated entirely as one word, the second term loses both its sense and its phonetic shape; it tends to be reduced to the value of a suffix. It is in this way that important German suffixes such as *-heit,* *-tum,* and *-lich* have been created. When the two terms keep their individuality, words can be formed in which the degree of fusion of the two terms is infinitely varied: in an everyday word like Ger. *Zeitschrift,* the two terms are only barely perceptible, while a new formation of this sort is understood only if one thinks explicitly of the two terms. Technical languages have in this process an unlimited resource for the creation of new words.

Chapter XVI

Some Nouns of Number

THE NUMBERING system can be used appropriately to illustrate how the Indo-European vocabulary has been altered in Germanic. Everything about it goes back to Indo-European through an unbroken tradition, and yet there are hardly any cases in which the common Indo-European forms are represented exactly.

In the rapid examination made here of a few forms, the words for numbers will be cited only in Gothic, unless there are special reasons for citing others.

The Indo-European stem *sem-, which meant 'one,' did not continue as a number, not even as the first member of a compound which it had been in Skr. sa-kŕt, 'one time,' or Lat. sim-plex. However, the form *sem- is well represented in Germanic; it is represented in Gothic by sama, 'the same,' samana, 'together,' simle, 'formerly,' and sums, 'somebody.' These forms, however, have nothing to do with numeration.

"One" is expressed in Gothic by ains, a word which originally meant 'alone.' Throughout the domain of Germanic, which extends from Baltic to Italo-Celtic, we observe a similar substitution: OPr. ains, Got. ains, OIr. ōen, and Lat. ūnus (representing oinos). Here we are in the presence of one of the important and numerous particularities of vocabulary, which are found throughout this same domain and not elsewhere. It is in these same languages, from Baltic to Italo-Celtic, that the action of "sowing," for example, is expressed by the root *sē- and that the word for "sea" is expressed by related words: OSl. morje, Got. marei, Ir. muir, and Lat. mare.

As for "first," we find, in the sense of Lat. prior, Got. fruma and OE. forma, and, in the sense of Lat. primus, Got. frumists and OE. fyrmest. Similar forms are found on the one hand in Lit. pìrmas, and on the other hand in Umbrian promom, that is, in the same domain where Got. ains has its correspondents. Greek has promos, but this is in the sense of 'one who is in the first rank, chief,' and Attic has oinos, oinē, but this is in the sense of 'ace' (of dice).

As often happens in languages where the nouns have lost the

grammatical category of the dual, the forms for "two" in Germanic have been replaced by plural forms; thus in Gothic we find *twai* (masc.), *twos* (fem.), and *twa* (neuter).

For the genitive, the language has utilized a form with geminated -*y*-, as Greek did for the multiplicative *doiós*, 'double' (from *dwoiyos), opposite Skr. *dvaydḥ* (with the same meaning). Thus, we find Got. *twaddje*, OI. *tueggia*, and OHG. *zweiio*. Lithuanian has likewise a gen. pl. *dvĕjŭ*, from *dwoiyōn.

The distributive is obtained by means of the suffix -*no*-, as in Lit. *dvynù*, 'two by two.' The Germanic form is based on *dwis, 'twice,' as in OI. *tuennr*, 'double,' which is like Lat. *bini*.

The same dialectal distribution is found in the use of related forms meaning "other" (with reference to a single term) to express the idea of "second": OSl. *vŭtorŭ*, Lit. *añtras*, Got. *anþar*, and, with -*l*- borrowed from *alius*, Lat. *alter*.

The Gothic words *sibun*, 'seven,' *niun*, 'nine,' and *taihun*, 'ten,' pose a problem: the final nasal cannot be explained by reference to the ancient final nasal vowel represented by the -*em* of Lat. *septem*, *nouem*, and *decem*, the -*a* of Gr. *heptá*, *ennéa*, and *déka*, and the -*a* of Skr. *saptá*, *ndva*, and *dáça*. In Gothic, -*u* final would be expected. The -*un* supposes an ancient *-*ṇd* (based on *-*ṃd* for "seven" and "ten"). The -*unt*- of Germanic appears in the genitive plural of the words for units of "ten": *sibunte-hund* ('seventy'), *niunte-hund* ('ninety'), and *taihunde-hund* ('one hundred'). It is this final dental which through dissimilation explains the early disappearance of the *t* of IE. *septṃ in all the Germanic languages: *sibun*, descended from *sibund, represents an ancient **septṃ't*.

In *sibun* and *niun* the final dental is analogous to that of *taihun*, which alone is etymological: we find it also in Lit. *dēšimt* and in OSl. *desęt*-. The proof that we must start from *dékṃt/*dékṃd is that in West Germanic we have the representation of a form *dekomd with vowel *o*: OHG. *zehan*, OS. *tehan*, and Northumbrian OE. *téa*. The contrast is the one shown between Beotian Gr. *wikati*, 'twenty,' and Gr. *triākonta*, 'thirty,' and between Arm. *kʼsan*, 'twenty,' and Arm. *eresun*, 'thirty,' that is, between *-(*d*)*kṃtĭ* and *-(*d*)*komt*. In Baltic and in Slavic the ancient invariable adjective "ten" disappeared and was replaced by the word for "a group of ten." In Germanic the facts are more complicated: the noun for the number "ten" is indeed, as in Slavic, the noun for "a group of ten." However, while the form -*un*(*t*) was extended to "seven" and "nine," the adjective value of Got. *sibun* and *niun* was maintained, as was the invariable character of these adjectives; and this adjective value along with the invariable character was extended to the noun for "a group of ten," which found itself thus filling a role similar to that of Lat. *decem*, Gr. *déka*, and so forth. Only the fixed form Got. *taihuntehund*, from which were formed *sibuntehund, niuntehund*, and even *ahtautehund*, keeps a trace of the ancient value of *taihun*.

The fact that "ten" is expressed by the noun "a group of ten" has had the same consequence in Germanic as it has had in Slavic and Baltic: the type of Gr. *triā-konta*, 'thirty,' or of Skr. *pancā-çát-* (acc. *pancā-çátam* and so on), 'fifty,' did not develop. The nouns for "tens" are then expressed by a noun of number followed by a full form of the noun for "a group of ten" with its inflection. Thus, "with twenty" is translated into Gothic as *mip twaim tigum*; in the accusative *prins tiguns* is 'thirty.' Unlike Got. *taihun* and OHG. *zehan*, which are ancient nominative-accusative neuters, these forms are masculine; the difference is similar to that which is found between the Greek type *triā-konta* (ancient nominative-accusative plural neuter) and Skr. *triṃçát-*, 'a group of thirty' (feminine). The Gothic here represents the common Germanic type. We have only to add that beside the form with vowel *e*, implied by Got. *tigu-*, there was a form with zero vocalism represented by forms such as OI. *tottogo*, 'twenty,' and *tugr*, 'a group of ten.' This is found also in the *a* of Arm. *tasn*, 'ten.'

Germanic is distinguished from Baltic and Slavic by the fact that the noun for "ten," *tigus*, in these forms does not come from **dekṃt-m-*. Some linguists have started from the form of the oblique case Got. **tigum* and so on, which may be based on **dekṃt-m-* (with an ending beginning with *-m-*). However, it is difficult to see why Germanic would have developed usual forms for the nominative and the accusative (as well as for the genitive) from the less usual forms of the dative-instrumental. Beside the common Indo-European **dek'omt-*, **dek'ṃt-* and **(d)k'omt-*, **(d)k'ṃt-* for 'a group of ten,' there was a West Indo-European form **dek'u-*, implied by Lat. *decu-ssis* and *decu-ria* and by Umbrian *tekv-ias*. It is then **dek'u-*, **d°kú-* which are represented by Germanic **tigu-*, **tugu* (it should be noted that the type **dekṃt-*, 'a group of ten,' is not represented in Italo-Celtic).

Gothic forms, Old Scandinavian forms, and certain survivals of Old English forms show that **tigu-*, **tugu-* were inflected. However, under the influence of the forms for "five" to "ten," the inflection tended everywhere to disappear. Already in Old Icelandic, the ancient dual *tottogo*, 'twenty,' which did not follow a normal inflectional pattern, had become invariable, while *prír tiger*, 'three groups of ten,' still maintained its inflection. The other groups were welded and subsequently became invariable. In Old High German, the welding and the absence of inflection of the word resulting from this welding were already manifest in the earliest texts, as in OHG. *zweinzug, dri-zug*, OS. *twēn-tig, thri-tig*, and so forth. At an early date, the substantive character of these nouns was shown by the fact that the numbered object was put in the genitive plural: OHG. *feorzug wehhōno*, 'four weeks,' and OS. *thritig jāro*, 'thirty years.' In time, the analogy of the first nouns of number prevailed, and the numbered object was put in the case called for by the role of the group in the sentence.

These peculiarities of nouns of number are doubly remarkable. On the one hand, we can see in them the dialectal position of Germanic among the Indo-European languages. In the form of Got. *taihun* and OHG. *zehan*, Germanic agrees with Slavic and Baltic, just as the noun for "thousand," Got. *þūsundi*, finds correspondents only in OPr. *tūsimtons* and OSl. *tysęšta*. In the form of **tigu-*, it agrees with Latin *decu-*. The noun for "one," Got. *ains*, is identical to those which we find in Baltic and Italo-Celtic.

On the other hand, the Germanic forms have had a rapid evolution, and the ancient stage of these forms cannot be distinguished on a cursory examination; if we did not know the Baltic and Slavic forms, the origin of Got. *taihun* and OHG. *zehan* would not be easily discernible. Although the most ancient texts reveal the original structure of nouns for "twenty," "thirty," and so on, these nouns tended early to conform to the type of nouns for "five," "six," and so on. Beginning with the earliest tradition, the forms of OHG. *zweinzug*, *drizug*, and so forth reached a stage which agrees with the modern type.

Conclusion to Part Three

IN ITS dialectal origins, the Germanic vocabulary is closer to the Baltic and Slavic vocabulary and to the Celtic and Italic vocabulary than to the Greek, Armenian, and Indo-Iranian vocabularies. When a Germanic word is found in only one other language, this language is one of the former. For example, the Gothic present *tiuha*, 'I pull,' is found only in Lat. *dūcō*, and the Gothic substantive *hals*, 'neck,' is found only in Lat. *collus, collum*; on the other hand, Got. *haims*, 'village,' is found only in OPr. *caymis* and Lit. *kaimas, kĕmas*, and Got. *hails*, 'in good health,' is found only in OSl. *cĕlŭ*, 'in good health' (with OPr. *kailūstikan*, 'health').

Although it conserves a number of terms from the aristocratic stock of the Indo-European vocabulary, Germanic, like Latin, has a number of words which seem to be of popular origin. Thus we find in it a great many forms with geminated interior consonants which in Indo-European are popular in origin; for example, parallel to Got. *bilaigon*, 'to lick,' West Germanic offers OHG. *lecchōn*, OS. *likkōn*, and OE. *liccian*. The formal noun for "earth," represented by Skr. *kṣam-* and Gr. *khthon-*, is replaced by the Gothic derivative *airþa* and so forth, which is from a word of more technical character that designates "cultivable soil"; the only trace of the formal noun for "earth" is found in the derivative *guma*, 'man,' literally 'terrestrial,' Lat. *homō*, and Lit. *žmû*, in opposition to "celestial" gods. At an early date, the civilization of the old Indo-European type tended to become eliminated in the Germanic world.

Many foreign influences are evident in the vocabulary; some items come from an unknown language such as the one to which Germanic owes the noun for "silver" (Got. *silubr*); for a time Celtic furnished some important words. With regard to certain words, like OE. *mearh*, OHG. *marah*, Welsh *march*, and Irish *marc*, 'horse,' we wonder whether Germanic and Celtic borrowed, perhaps independently, from an unknown language to whose influence they were both subjected. Then came the influence of classical civilization in Latin form, especially in the Rhine region, and in Greek form. It is from Gr. *kyrikē*, doubtlessly as early as the fourth century, that the language of Christians took the West Germanic name for "church": OHG. *kiricha, kirika* and OE. *cirice*. While Got. *hails* and the derived verb *hailjan*, 'to heal,' are old Germanic words, it was to translate Lat. *salutare* that such words as OHG. *heilazen* and OE. *hālettan* were formed. We can see here how from early times the Germanic vocabulary became penetrated with Greco-Latin elements, either by direct borrowing or by the absorption in Germanic words of meanings found in words of the languages of civilization which influenced the Germanic world.

General Conclusion

COMMON GERMANIC, made up almost entirely of Indo-European elements and with many Indo-European traits still in its grammar, was already in reality a new system. By developing innovations which it presented, the dialects in which it became differentiated have ultimately tended toward an ever greater remoteness from Indo-European. Even the most conservative group, the German group, has a grammar quite different from Indo-European grammar and a vocabulary penetrated with foreign words and with foreign meanings for words. In areas where historical circumstances have hastened the development, almost nothing has remained of the Indo-European type of language: in English the pronunciation is notably different, the grammar is of a type which is the farthest possible from the Indo-European type, and the vocabulary contains very few terms with their ancient meanings. English is linked to Indo-European by a historical continuity, but it has kept almost nothing of the Indo-European type.

Each of the Indo-European languages shows an autonomous development of the common initial language. In each one we notice special tendencies which reflect in some measure usages peculiar to earlier languages which the Indo-European languages have replaced. Nowhere are these original developments more clearly recognizable than in Germanic. Nowhere else do we perceive more clearly tendencies which seem to come from some earlier language. Nowhere else can we see better how the ancient Indo-European vocabulary has been altered, enriched, and adapted to the new needs of civilization.

Bibliography

In a little book like this, it would not be possible to give even briefly a complete bibliography of works relative to Germanic languages. It will suffice to indicate a few works in which one will find, with a more extensive bibliography, the means of completing the very brief indications given in the present work.

The best orientation on general linguistics is furnished by the *Cours de linguistique générale* by F. de Saussure, 2nd ed. (Paris, 1922); *Langage* by J. Vendryes (Paris, 1921); *Language* by E. Sapir (New York, 1921); and *Language* by O. Jespersen (London, 1922).

For descriptive phonetics, various manuals are available, notably: L. Roudet, *Éléments de phonétique générale* (Paris, 1910); H. Sweet, *A Primer of Phonetics* (Oxford, 1906); P. Passy, *Petite phonétique comparée des principales langues européennes* (Leipzig, 1906); and O. Jespersen, *Lehrbuch der Phonetik* (Leipzig, 1913).

On comparative grammar in general, there is only one great manual, *Grundriss der vergleichenden Grammatik der indogermanischen Sprachen*, by K. Brugmann and B. Delbrück, 2nd ed. (Strasbourg, 1897–1911); an abridgment of this work, *Kurze vergleichende Grammatik*, by K. Brugmann, has been translated into French under the title *Abrégé de grammaire comparée* (Paris, 1905).

An outline of the principles of comparative grammar will be found in A. Meillet, *Introduction à l'étude comparative des langues indo-européennes*, 8th ed. (Paris, 1937).

For the comparative grammar of Germanic in particular, one may consult in French the *Précis de grammaire comparée de l'anglais et de l'allemand*, 2nd ed. (Paris, 1907) by V. Henry. In German, one may consult G. Loewe, *Germanische Sprachwissenschaft*, 2 vols., 4th ed. (Berlin and Leipzig, 1918); F. Kluge, *Urgermanisch, Vorgeschichte der altgermanischen Dialekte* (Strasbourg, 1913; this is one of the volumes of the third edition of *Grundriss der germanischen Philologie*); W. A. Streitberg, *Urgermanische Grammatik* (Heidelberg, 1896); F. Dieter, *Laut- und Formenlehre der altgermanischen Dialekte* (Leipzig, 1903); W. Wilmanns, *Deutsche Grammatik* (Strasbourg, 1899–1911); and R. C. Boer, *Oorgermaansch Handboek* (Harlem, 1918).

On the history of the various German dialects, the volumes of the *Grundriss der germanischen Philologie*, the third edition of which is composed of separate fascicles, should be consulted, as should the collections of grammars. There are two main collections. One is edited by W. Braune and published by Niemeyer at Halle; especially to be noted are the grammars of Old English by E. Sievers, of Old High German by W. Braune, and of Old Icelandic and of Old Swedish by A. Noreen. The other is edited by W. A. Streitberg and published by Winter at Heidelberg; especially to be noted are the *Gotisches Elementarbuch* by W. A. Streitberg and the *Althochdeutsches Lesebuch für Anfänger* by J. Mansion (Heidelberg, 1932), which is clear and easy to use. See also *Althochdeutsche Grammatik* and *Althochdeutsches*

Lesebuch by H. Naumann (which are two volumes from the collection Göschen). Beginners will find it useful to get their bearings with little books such as *Unser Deutsch* by F. Kluge (collection *Wissenschaft und Bildung*); *Die deutschen Mundarten* by H. Reis and *Plattdeutsche Mundarten* by H. Grimme (collection Göschen). In French, noteworthy works are *Histoire de la langue allemande* by H. Lichtenberger (Paris, 1895) and *Phonétique allemande* by Piquet (Paris, 1907). For English it will be found profitable to study the works of O. Jespersen, notably *Growth and Structure of the English Language*, 2nd ed. (Leipzig, 1912), and *Chapters on English* (London, 1918). The *Petite histoire de l'anglais* by H. C. Wyld exists in an augmented English edition (1927).

As for etymology, there is no overall exposé of Germanic etymology; one can use with caution the *Wortschatz der germanischen Spracheinheit* by H. Falk and A. Torp (third volume of the fourth edition of the *Etymologisches Wörterbuch* by A. Fick). The *Etymologisches Wörterbuch der deutschen Sprache* by F. Kluge, 9th ed. (Berlin, 1921) is an excellent book, as is the second edition of J. Franck's *Etymologisch woordenboek der nederlandsche taal* by N. van Wijk (The Hague, 1912). For Gothic see the second edition of the *Kurzgefasstes etymologisches Wörterbuch der gotischen Sprache* by C. Uhlenbeck and especially the second edition of the *Etymologisches Wörterbuch der gotischen Sprache* by S. Feist (Halle, 1923), which is good. For Scandinavian we have the *Etymologisk Ordbok over det norske og det danske sprog* by H. Falk and A. Torp (Kristiania, 1903–1906), of which there is a German translation (published by Winter at Heidelberg); and the *Svensk etymologisk ordbok* by E. Hellquist (Lund, 1922).

As for the prehistory of Germanic, of special interest is S. Feist, *Indogermanen und Germanen*, 3rd ed. (Halle, 1926).

Annual bibliography is available in the *Jahresbericht über die Erscheinungen auf dem Gebiete der germanischen Philologie* (Leipzig, since 1880), and since 1914 in the *Indogermanisches Jahrbuch* published by the *Indogermanische Gesellschaft*.

INDEX

Index